WHY WON'T MY TEENAGER TALK TO ME?

Second Edition

John Coleman

LONDON AND NEW YORK

Second edition published 2019
by Routledge
2 Park Square, Milton Park, Abingdon, Oxon OX14 4RN

and by Routledge
711 Third Avenue, New York, NY 10017

Routledge is an imprint of the Taylor & Francis Group, an informa business

First edition published by Routledge 2014

British Library Cataloguing-in-Publication Data
A catalogue record for this book is available from the British Library

Library of Congress Cataloging-in-Publication Data
Names: Coleman, John C. (John Christopher), 1940– author.
Title: Why won't my teenager talk to me? / Dr John Coleman.
Description: 2nd Edition. | New York, NY : Routledge, 2019.
| Revised edition of the author's Why won't my teenager talk
to me?, 2014.
Identifiers: LCCN 2018024255 (print) | LCCN 2018026632 (ebook) |
ISBN 9781317702825 (Adobe) | ISBN 9781317702818 (ePub) |
ISBN 9781317702801 (Mobipocket) | ISBN 9781138560468 (hardback)
| ISBN 9781138560475 (pbk.) | ISBN 9781315780542 (ebook)
Subjects: LCSH: Parent and teenager. | Adolescence. | Parenting.
Classification: LCC HQ799.15 (ebook) | LCC HQ799.15 .
C633 2019 (print) | DDC 306.874–dc23
LC record available at https://lccn.loc.gov/2018024255

ISBN: 978-1-138-56046-8 (hbk)
ISBN: 978-1-138-56047-5 (pbk)
ISBN: 978-0-203-71158-3 (ebk)

Typeset in Sabon
by Wearset Ltd, Boldon, Tyne and Wear

Due Date	Due Date	Due Date

Do
peni
wor
bedi
conc
Wh?
insig
ful t
T
abou
bool
this
brair
side
Cole
socia
C
talki
ways
fami
siona
healt

Dr J   psychologist, and was formerly a Senior Research Fellow at the University of Oxford. He is the Founder of a research centre studying adolescents and their families, and during his career he has also run a special school for troubled teenagers and worked as a policy advisor for Government. In addition to running workshops for parents of teenagers, he has created two series for TV, and written books and developed videos on the adolescent years. John's pioneering work has been widely recognised, and in the Queen's Birthday Honours in 2001 he was awarded an OBE for services to young people.

"This book merges the voices of parents and teenagers with Dr Coleman's authoritative, well-defined framework, offering practical information and advice for parents of today's teenagers." **Janey Downshire, Teenagers Translated, UK**

"John writes in a generous, practical and informed manner about difficult subject areas. He provides a frame work 'STAGE' for reflection and reference, but most of all an open-minded approach to get the most out parenting during the teenage years – he even allows us to consider that this can be a wonderful and not terrible experience because he talks to both parents and teenagers themselves." **Jez Todd, CEO of Family Lives, UK**

"In today's pressured and competitive world, it seems that parents have much to worry about and too little sensible guidance. Parents are full of questions, for their experiences are new to them and, in the case of the fast-changing digital world, new to everyone. John Coleman's years of expertise, sound research and sympathetic vision allows him to offer wise yet practical answers in a lively, accessible and thoroughly up-to-date manner." **Professor Sonia Livingstone OBE, London School of Economics and Political Science, UK**

"This book is essential reading for anyone with a teenager. Fostering and maintaining good communication with a teenager can feel impossible – conversations end up turning into arguments and everyone starts to feel worried or upset. This book gives parents the insights they need to keep family communication channels open. It's insightful and practical and should be on every parent's bookshelf." **Vicki Shotbolt, Founder and CEO of Parent Zone, UK**

"This is the book that every parent of a teenager should have on their bedside table. Read it through, dip in and out – it contains so much that can help you. Coleman combines wisdom and sympathy with practicality and facts. He gives tips and suggestions on how to talk to your teenagers, and how to listen. But far more important, he gives you insight into why your teenagers act and feel the way they do and dissects the increasing pressures they come under in today's world. This new edition contains the latest research on the teenage brain." **Suzie Hayman, Agony Aunt for *Woman* Magazine and Trustee of the charity Family Lives**

CONTENTS

FOREWORD TO THE
2ND EDITION

It has been rewarding to learn that so many people – parents and practitioners – have found the first edition of this book a helpful guide to understanding teenagers.

So much has changed in the last five years since the book first appeared. Our knowledge of the human brain has increased, with new research findings appearing all the time. A significant amount of this new research has concerned adolescence, and these insights have been incorporated into the book, with a whole chapter devoted to the changing teenage brain.

I put forward the notion of a STAGE framework in the first edition of this book, and I am delighted that it has been received with enthusiasm by social workers and other professionals. Undoubtedly it needs more work, and some more formal evaluation would be a sensible next step. Up to this point it has been used in group work with parents, in telephone counselling and in short-term therapeutic work with troubled parents. It has also been incorporated into support programmes for foster carers. In this edition I have expanded the ideas, and included a short section at the start of all the chapters in Part II illustrating how the STAGE framework can apply to topics such as health, the digital world, friendship and the peer group, and so on.

The social world of the teenager has continued to change over the last five years. Three particular issues come to mind, and these have been incorporated into this edition. The first has to do with the impact of social media. Commentators and policy makers believe that this is a serious challenge for young people, and worry about the long-term consequences. As for young people themselves, most of the research appears to indicate that they worry less, and are more likely to point to the positive opportunities afforded by smart phones and access to the internet.

The second issue has to do with mental health. Studies do seem to show that there has been an increase in mental health problems for some groups and in some aspects of behaviour. Those most affected would appear to be girls who demonstrate self-harming behaviour. However, it is important to note that we still lack reliable research data on this topic. In addition, it is generally accepted that services in the UK have been badly affected by government cuts to funding. As waiting times for treatment increase, it is hardly surprising that young people suffer for longer and experience greater levels of distress.

The third issue has to do with gender. In the last five years there has been a remarkable shift in attitudes to gender. The term "gender neutral" is in widespread use, and many are arguing that gender is no longer a binary concept. The conflicts over school toilets illustrate this in graphic form. Many teenagers wonder about their gender, and the numbers who describe themselves as "trans" or "transyouth" appear to be growing from year to year. It is not surprising that adults worry when confronted with a young person who wishes to change gender. However, this is clearly an important trend in adolescent identity development. It is a topic that needs to be dealt with carefully and sensitively by parents, carers, and professionals.

I would like to end by thanking my publisher, and most particularly my editor, Lucy Kennedy, for their continued support and assistance. I have been lucky to be able to work with Lucy and her team at Routledge.

John Coleman
May 2018

Part I

1

THE TEENAGE YEARS

Are you proud of your daughter, but wish she would tell you more about what is happening in her life? Are you worried about your son, who is spending more and more time in his bedroom? Are you a foster carer who wants to understand the silence of the teenager who has just come to live with you?

The teenage years are a time of concern for parents and carers from all backgrounds. This book aims to address these concerns, and to offer new ideas about how relationships can be managed and improved where necessary. The book has a focus on communication. There is a strong reason for this. Being able to communicate with your teenager is the key to good relationships. If parents and teenagers can talk to each other, it will be easier to manage the ups and downs of family life. Things will be a lot harder if channels of communication close down during this stage. As one father put it to me: "I'd say the golden rule for parents is: conversation, not confrontation!".

One of the main reasons I called this book: *Why Won't My Teenager Talk to Me?* is that this is a question so often asked when parents of teenagers come together in a group. I have run many groups for parents of young people, and I am always surprised at how often adults believe that communication with their teenager has broken down.

Parents experience a sense that the teenager no longer wishes to talk to them. They believe young people would prefer to talk to their friends. They see that the teenager is intent on pushing them away. This may involve putting a PRIVATE sign on the bedroom door, a refusal to engage in any conversation, or a preoccupation with the messages that are coming in on the smart phone.

When I ask teenagers about this topic they say that communication with parents consists of one of two things. Either they are being

3

interrogated, or they are being nagged about something they have not done yet, such as their homework. Of course this is not a good basis for communication! I will have a lot more to say about all this later in the book, but, for the moment, here are some initial thoughts about communication:

- Your teenager will talk, but not always at the time of your choosing.
- Your teenager will talk, but not about the things that he or she considers to be private.
- Your teenager will talk, but not if there is a sense that the talk might turn into an interrogation.
- Your teenager will talk, but not if there is a feeling that you are busy, distracted, or likely to be interrupted.

What is the reason for all this? There are particular things about the adolescent stage of life that have a direct impact on communication. First, there are times when teenagers feel that they need to be in control. They will talk, but at their own time, and in their own way. This is partly to do with lack of confidence, but also to do with confusing emotions. Both these factors mean that it is not always easy to talk openly just at the point when a parent wants to have a discussion about something.

Second, it is important to recognise that during these years young people do need a degree of privacy to work things out for themselves. They want to be independent individuals, growing and maturing into adults. No one who is trying to be independent will feel like telling their parents everything that is happening to them. Here is one 15-year-old girl's view of the situation:

> My Mum often says to me: "Why don't you talk about your problems?" I say: "I do, I just don't talk to you. I talk to my friends." I have talked to my Mum about things, but not at the time they are happening. I tell her about things after they have happened, after I've sorted it out for myself what's happening. I still think she wants me to tell her, but I can't.

This gives a helpful insight into how a girl might think about talking to her mother. She will talk, but in her time, and after she has sorted things out in her own mind.

Here are some further thoughts about communication between parents and teenagers.

- Communication is a two-way process. It involves listening as well as talking. The more you show you are listening, the more likely it is that the teenager will want to talk to you.
- Communication is a skill. It is something you have to learn. Young people sometimes hang back because they feel that adults are better at communication than they are.
- Communication is much more than the words that come out of your mouth. The message you send will be affected by the way you stand, the gestures you make, and the emotion that is conveyed. It's not only what you say, but also how you say it that matters most.
- A lot of communication today takes place on-line. Young people may feel just as comfortable sending a text or messaging than talking face-to-face. Communication can occur in many different media.

Some important themes are already emerging which will run throughout the book. The teenage years represent a stage in the process of growing up. This means that there are particular behaviours, attitudes, and emotions which are a part of the teenage years. These will all change markedly as the young person grows older and moves towards adulthood.

In the book there will also be a strong emphasis on the fact that relationships go two ways. This is illustrated by the fact that talking and listening go hand in hand. However, it goes further than that. It sounds obvious, but the family is like a system. Each person influences the other. How your teenager behaves will have an impact on you; however, you too are playing your part. What you do, and how you behave, has a direct influence on how your teenager behaves. In this book I will be referring often to the importance of understanding the two-way nature of relationships between parent and teenager.

Why this book?

Although communication plays a big role in this book, there are many equally important topics to be covered here. The world of the teenager is changing almost in front of our eyes. The pressures of the education system, new family structures, changing gender identities, and the opportunities and threats associated with the digital world are all posing challenges for both teenagers and their parents today. New research on the brain, mental health, digital romance, nutrition and eating behaviours, sleep, and learning are all having an effect on our understanding of how young people are growing up today. This book should help parents and carers learn something of what it is like to be a teenager in the twenty-first century. Here you will find both a framework for understanding this particular stage of life, as well as a guide to some new thinking about adolescent development.

This book is for all parents and carers of teenagers. It is for those who are thinking about the arrival of puberty, and wondering about the changes that they will experience in the family in the coming years. It is for those who are struggling with the "attitude" of a 14- or 15-year-old. These boys and girls will be trying to establish their own independence and show their parents that they can manage on their own. It is for those who are worried about the impact of social media, and struggle to know how to react to the constant use of smart phones and other devices.

This book is for parents who are facing divorce or separation. They will be looking for advice about how to support and protect their teenagers from the effects of these changes. It is also for those who have serious worries about their teenagers, whether these are to do with bullying, sex, peer pressure, eating disorders, drugs and alcohol, or teenage pregnancy. Most important of all, this is a book:

- to help you navigate the teenage years,
- to help you become a resilient parent,
- to help you talk, and listen, to your teenager.

Being a parent of a teenager can be tough. One mother I talked to put it like this.

> It's very difficult to learn to be a parent of a teenager. It's the most under-rated job in the world. It's easier to be a brain surgeon than to be a really good parent!

Most families who were interviewed as a background to this book mentioned some challenges associated with the teenage years. Some parents were sad at the loss of a close relationship with their son or daughter. Others were angry about the constant arguments and rejection of parental advice. However, it is also important to say that many parents found these years rewarding. They pointed to the energy and the enthusiasm of their teenagers. Although they may have experienced irritation, conflict, and worry too, they were able to find rewards in seeing their children gradually move to a more adult stage of life.

Yet no one finds it easy to be a parent of a teenager. What is the right way to be a parent at this stage? How strict or easy-going should you be? What is the best way to support a teenager who is pushing you away? What do you do if homework is being ignored, or if a young person is up half the night on the phone or internet? What is the best way to communicate with someone who seems not to be listening?

> It's frustrating because you want to advise them, but they don't really want to know. And I suppose it's that learning that in some ways they've just got to learn by their own mistakes, but you don't really want them to make mistakes, so you try to protect them from that. But at the same time you've got to let them get on with it.
>
> (Mother of three teenagers)

This mother gets to the heart of every parent's dilemma: when to step in, and when to hold back? You may be clear about the role of a parent in the early years, but how should you manage the teenage years? This is a dilemma I will explore in detail in later chapters.

There are three important elements to this book. These are:

- an original framework for parenting teenagers,
- the voices of parents themselves,
- new insights into topics such as brain development, sleep, social media, gender identity, and other important topics.

An original framework for parenting

In Chapters 3 to 8 of this book I will be outlining an original framework for parenting that will be helpful for those living with teenagers. The ideas behind the framework all stem from highly respected research findings. I call this framework "STAGE".

I have given the framework this name because I want to emphasise the point that the teenage years are a process, a time of change and development. Things will alter gradually over time, and the difficult stage – if it is a difficult stage – will not last forever. There are also particular features of this stage that make it different from any other.

Another reason for calling it "STAGE" is because each of the letters in the word STAGE represents a different aspect of parenting.

S stands for the Significance of parents. Parents of teenagers are the most significant people in the life of the young person. Parents may think they are not important any more, but their role is absolutely crucial. Parents of teenagers matter just as much as parents of younger children, they just matter in a different way.

T stands for Two-way communication. As I have noted, communication between parents and teenagers is a two-way process. Parents may think they are the ones who need to do the talking, but listening is just as important. Young people have as much influence as adults in determining how each communicates with the other. Both adults and young people play their part. Recognising and taking account of this two-way process will help to achieve improved communication.

A stands for Authority. One of the most difficult aspects of parenting is to know how to exercise parental authority. What boundaries and structures are needed for teenagers? Should punishment be used, and if so, what punishments make sense? How is it possible to retain parental authority, while letting go at the same time? I will be suggesting what is called "authoritative parenting" as the most appropriate way to exercise authority.

G stands for Generation gap. I include this idea because each generation of teenagers has a different set of challenges and pressures to deal with. It is easy for parents to assume that what was right for them will also be right for their children. However, things are very different today compared with 40 years ago. As a result, young people of this generation have to make different choices from those made by their parents.

E stands for Emotion. Emotion plays an important part in affecting relationships between parents and teenagers. Whether it is anxiety, anger, sadness, regret, envy, or guilt, all these feelings influence how parents manage the situation with teenagers. Being aware of your feelings, and finding ways of dealing with them, are important steps on the way to having better relationships in the family.

This is a very brief introduction to the ideas behind "STAGE". All the ideas contained within the framework can lead to more effective parenting, and to better relationships between you and your teenager. The first half of this book will be devoted to outlining the framework. This is an original way of thinking about parenting during the teenage years.

The voices of parents

Before writing this book, I arranged for interviews to be carried out with parents of teenagers in many different circumstances. Both mothers and fathers were included, as well as step-parents and foster carers. Parents from different ethnic backgrounds talked to us, as did those having serious problems with their teenage sons and daughters. The voices of these parents have been used as much as possible throughout the book. I will also include the views of some teenagers. A group of young people were asked their thoughts on parents, on friends, and on what it is like to be a teenager today. Where appropriate I will add in their voices too.

Why is this important? There are three good reasons for including the views of parents and teenagers in this book. The first will be obvious already. Even the few quotes used so far pinpoint experiences that make us all feel: "I know just what she means!" Parents' voices will help readers to engage with this book, and bring what happens in real families to the page.

Second, some parents who attend parenting groups report that they feel alone and isolated. They believe that their teenager is the worst ever, that no parent can be going through such a bad time. And when they hear other parents talk in the group they are surprised, and re-assured, to find that other families are just the same. They learn that they are not alone, and that the problems they are facing are the same as those faced by many other parents. Being able to read about the experiences of other parents in this book should help in much the same way.

Third, it is useful to learn how other parents have managed. They will have practical suggestions to make, and be able to reflect on their experiences. I will make use of these experiences, and draw on them to explore what it is like living with teenagers. The intention of this book is to help you navigate the teenage years. The experiences of real families will be a valuable part of this process.

New research

Over the last 10 years or so some important and useful information from research on teenagers has become available. I want to make sure that this research forms part of the book. This new knowledge about teenagers can help us understand them better. Even more important, we can make use of this information to develop practical ideas about how to manage family life with a teenager.

Throughout the book I will mention what I consider to be important new knowledge about adolescence. At this point I will mention just three examples to give you a sense of what I mean. The first example has to do with the adolescent brain. The development of scanning techniques has made it possible to learn what happens in the brain at different stages of life. One of the most striking results stemming from the use of these new techniques is the conclusion that there is rapid and fundamental change in the brain during the teenage years. This has major implications for understanding behaviour, and has helped us make sense of some of the more puzzling features of adolescence.

A second example has to do with sleep. It has been quite an eye-opener to discover that the hormones that control sleep patterns are not the same in adolescence as they are in children or adults. If young people liked to stay up late at night, or resisted getting up in the morning, parents tended to put this down to teenagers just being difficult. Now we have learnt that there is a biological reason why teenage sleep patterns are different from those of other age groups.

Recent research has also highlighted that sleep plays an important role in learning and memory. The brain remains active during sleep, and much of what has happened during the day is processed and consolidated at night. This finding has emphasised just how important good sleep is for young people. They are at a period in their lives when learning is a key activity. Exam performance matters today more than it ever has, and so getting enough sleep can really make all the difference.

The last example I will choose here has to do with the way teenagers manage communication between themselves and their parents. Fascinating research on what is called "information management" has shown how teenagers make decisions about what to share with parents and what to hold back. This research helps to underline the fact that communication is a two-way process. If we are looking for ways of improving communication between parents and teenagers, then the results of research on "information management" will be of great help.

Negative attitudes to teenagers

A striking thing about teenagers is that they are often seen in a very negative light. Many adults expect teenagers to cause problems. They are perceived as trouble, and naturally this has an influence on how adults and young people relate to each other. One mother expressed it like this:

> It seems to me that people make a whole host of assumptions about teenagers. When I tell people I have teenage children they assume I must have problems.

Another mother explained how her husband had feared the worst.

> My husband, he kept talking about "Oooh! We'll see what happens when she turns into a teenager". He was always going: "Oh God, what's going to happen?". And he was almost coming from a place of anticipating the worst, and almost creating an illusion of a bad situation, you know. And she actually said to him: "I really hate it when I hear you talking to other grown-ups about teenagers, and it's almost like you're expecting me to become bad!".

Attitudes such as this interfere with good relationships. They also interfere with communication. If you start by believing that a teenager is going to cause a problem, it is more difficult to have a sensible conversation. Thinking about our attitudes to teenagers is the first step on the road to easier and better communication.

Conclusion: why talking matters

It is probably an obvious thing to say, but talking matters because effective parenting is not possible without it. If communication is difficult you will not be able to find out what matters to your teenager. You will not be able to discover what your teenager thinks is important or what your teenager is worried about. You will not be able to say that he or she is special for you, that you care about what is happening, that you love your teenager. Perhaps most important of all, you will not be able to find out what your teenager needs at his or her particular age and stage.

Many parents find talking to teenagers difficult. Because adults want to know what is happening, they tend to ask questions. "How did you get on at school today?", "What happened at your friend's house?", "How was the party last night?" To a teenager this may seem like interrogation, and no one likes being interrogated.

I have already pointed out that listening is as important as talking. However, it is not always clear how to listen. You cannot just say: "OK, here I am. I am listening now. What do you want to say?". That is obviously ridiculous. So how is it best to talk and listen?

I will have a lot more to say about this later, but for the present here are five things to think about as you read through the book.

- Timing. Choose your time. You will know when a young person feels like talking, and when they don't. In a car, or late at night are often good times to talk. Be guided by the teenager. Hold back when it does not feel right, and be patient. Rest assured that there will be times when your teenager will want to talk.

- Useful hooks. It is sometimes possible to use hooks like news items, events that are occurring in soap operas, or films or TV programmes to start a discussion. Talking about things that are happening to other people outside the home may be easier than talking about more personal things.
- Share. Be willing to talk about yourself. People often find it easier to talk if the other person discloses a little about themselves. Rather than asking the other person a direct question about themselves, you could try talking a little about what is happening to you. This will enable the other person to open up, and share something with you.
- Act. Sometimes actions can help to make communication easier. Offering to make a young person a snack or a cup of tea may be a better way to start a conversation than asking a direct question.
- Listen. Communication goes two ways. Talking and listening go hand in hand. The more you show you are listening, the more the other person will talk.

You will find more ideas about communication and further suggestions for ways to talk to your teenager in Chapter 5, and in the final chapter of the book. Before I get to these ideas I will spend some time outlining the physical and emotional changes that young people experience. In the next chapter I will discuss the changing brain.

The more adults understand what happens in the brain at this time, the easier it will be to manage relationships. Having a good sense of what underpins the growing up process is an essential part of effective parenting.

2

THE CHANGING BRAIN

The years of change

It could be said that the teenage years are basically a period of change. This is a period in life when the individual moves from being a child to being an adult. The only problem is that this process takes a long, long time to complete. There may be times when the young person becomes impatient. He or she may wish to become grown up overnight. On the other hand, there could also be times when the teenager feels that it is all moving too fast. There may be moments of feeling lonely and unsupported. It is then that the safe world of childhood can look quite attractive.

All teenagers are aware that change is happening. Puberty is one obvious example, and all young people experience the changes to their bodies as part of growing up. Other changes will be going on at the same time, such as moving from one school to another. There are changes in friendships and in the way parents and teenagers get on with one another.

When asked about change most young people say that life is more stressful now than it was in childhood. Most agree that getting to sleep is harder, and that moodiness can be a problem. These are things that pretty well everyone experiences.

Other changes will be true of some people, but not for everyone. One person might say that she is more influenced by friends now than she was before moving to secondary school. Another person may find school work much more difficult. However, not everyone has these experiences. For some young people their health or appearance becomes a concern, but again this is not the case for all teenagers.

The conclusion is that change is happening for everyone, but each young people will experience this in a slightly different way. These are all changes that individuals are aware of, that they can talk about. But what about the invisible changes in the brain that young people are not aware of? It is now time to consider these changes, and to look at how they affect the teenage years.

The invisible brain

As background it is important for you to know that up to the end of the twentieth century it was assumed that there was little further development in the brain after the end of childhood. We now know that this is quite untrue. In fact there is more change in the brain during adolescence than at any other time in human development apart from the first three years of life. This means that the teenage years are a critical period. What happens during this period has major implications for later development.

Of course the brain does not develop in isolation. The brain and the environment interact, each influencing each other. In this chapter I will describe the changes that occur in the teenage brain. I will show how these changes affect behaviour. I will also outline, at the end of the chapter, how you can use this knowledge to encourage healthy brain development. The more you understand what happens in the brain at this time, the more you can help teenagers manage this period of transition.

I should emphasise that the brain is immensely complex. The human brain is the most complex thing in nature. There are in the region of 100 billion nerve cells in the brain. During the teenage years, as I have said, the brain undergoes substantial change. There is growth and maturation in all areas of the brain. This is something we have learnt as a result of the technology of scanning.

The maturation of the brain allows for new learning and the development of new intellectual skills. In addition, the bridge between the two halves of the brain strengthens, allowing for greater connectivity, enabling the brain to use its capacity better. The material that encases the nerve fibres – called myelin – is also strengthened, so that messages can travel faster and more effectively around the brain.

A further change that occurs in late childhood is a significant increase in the amount of grey matter. This is the area of the brain in which most of the nerve cells are to be found. The grey matter is then gradually reorganised and re-arranged during the teenage years. The network of cells that are useful are reinforced, and the networks that are of little use are allowed to die away. This process is known as pruning. The phrase "use it or lose it" may be familiar to you. It means that connections between cells that are valuable should be developed and rehearsed.

Certain areas of the brain are particularly important

Two areas of the brain play a big part in the overall change that is happening during these years. These are the prefrontal cortex and the amygdala. Both these areas undergo very significant development at this time. The prefrontal cortex is the area most associated with thinking, planning, and problem-solving. The amygdala is the area associated with emotion, sensation, and arousal.

There are also areas in the brain associated with pleasure seeking, and these are more active during the teenage years. All these centres in the brain undergo significant alteration during these years. The brain is maturing, but this does not happen overnight. It takes a long time for all parts of the brain to function well together.

In some young people the amygdala may develop at a faster rate than the prefrontal cortex, and this is sometimes considered to be an explanation for risky behaviour. There may be times when some teenagers simply do not think ahead and do not take into account the consequences of their actions. In these circumstances the parts of the brain associated with pleasure and rewards can, for a time, prove to be more powerful than the areas linked to thinking and reasoning.

A third area of the brain which is important to mention is the hippocampus, the site in the brain most associated with memory. The hippocampus is the centre that processes and encodes memory traces, and is also associated with the retrieval of memories. It is especially active in adolescence, and plays an important role in learning.

Hormones

It has always been known that the teenage years are a time of significant change in the balance of hormones in the body. This upset in the hormone balance is often seen as an explanation for moody or irritable behaviour. What is new in our knowledge is that the balance of hormones affects brain development. The alterations and fluctuations of hormones act on various parts of the brain that have already been mentioned, such as the amygdala and the prefrontal cortex.

High levels of sex hormones, such as testosterone and progesterone, have an impact not only on the development of the sex organs, but they also lead to changes in behaviour. Surges of these hormones may encourage teenagers to seek out emotionally charged experiences, or to look for novelty and excitement.

It is worth noting that levels of hormones such as cortisol and serotonin fluctuate considerably during this period. The release of cortisol is linked to experiences of anxiety, whereas serotonin helps moderate anxiety. If these hormones are in flux, it will be apparent that emotions may be difficult to manage.

Lastly, it is important to mention dopamine. This is a hormone which is released when we get pleasure or enjoyment from an activity. The brain is particularly sensitive to dopamine during the teenage years, and some risky or thrill-seeking behaviours can be explained by increased dopamine activity at this time.

How do these changes affect the young person?

As the brain becomes more mature, new skills develop. Language is a good example. During the teenage years vocabulary gradually grows larger. This means that the young person will have more words at their fingertips when they are writing essays and completing projects. It also means that in conversation, with friends and with adults, they will get better at expressing their views and become more confident in their communication skills.

> I definitely feel, with my friends at least, that I can be more free with what I say. Like I have more ideas, more thoughts come into my head. With my parents it is harder, like they always seem to know what to say and I don't!

Memory is another example of something that is changing for the better. Although schools do not regularly test memory, we do know from research that memory capacity slowly increases during the teenage years. This is essential as the curriculum gets harder and exams loom larger in the life of the young person.

Another new skill that becomes available as people get older is the ability to think in abstract terms and to reason in a scientific manner. Being able to manage the science curriculum depends on being able to carry out scientific experiments and test alternative hypotheses. Teenagers begin to see that the world is a complicated place, and they are able to take into account the views of other people. "I used to think that things were either right or wrong. Now I can see that there are many shades of grey".

The development of all these skills is a direct result of the maturing of the prefrontal cortex and other areas of the brain related to thinking and cognition. However, as everyone is aware, it is not all straightforward. Some of the changes in the brain mean that this period in life has its downs as well as its ups. Take the thinking skills

I have just mentioned. The ability to understand the views of other people also means that the teenager can start thinking about how he or she looks to other people. Many teenagers become preoccupied with how they appear to other people, and what other people think of them.

This, then, is a period of great self-consciousness. New thinking skills lead to new thoughts about what the individual looks like to the rest of the world. For a while this can be quite unsettling. Gradually, however, young people will become more self-confident. They begin to feel more comfortable in their own skin, and come to accept the changes to their bodies and to their identities.

I mentioned the increase and then slow pruning of grey matter. This involves a substantial reorganisation in the way the brain is working. It is not surprising, therefore, that teenagers do feel some degree of confusion at times as the brain is adjusting to the pruning process. This confusion can take many forms. Some teenagers may feel they just have too many thoughts in their head at one time. They may feel unsure how to react to something on social media. They may find they are being asked to do things which make them feel uncomfortable. Or they may find that it is hard to make decisions about things that really matter. All these experiences, and many others, may be part of a reaction to what is going on in the brain at this time. "I wish I knew what I wanted, but I just don't. There's so many choices, and, like, how can I decide?"

Emotion is another aspect of life that is affected by the brain. Most teenagers find that, at times, their emotions swing from one extreme to the other. Many young people describe the sensation of having different emotions all muddled up together. Someone can be sad and happy, all in one day. It can be surprising how emotional individuals can get over little things. Managing feelings at this time can be tricky. This too is unsettling, and has an effect on relationships. "Moody? Yes definitely. I'm very emotional, me. Up and down, round and round! Slamming doors? Yes! I'm probably driving everyone in my family crazy."

Another thing that sometimes gets lost during this stage is a sense of proportion. If one bad thing happens a teenager may have the sense that the world is coming to an end. Everything, even trivial things, can seem very immediate and important. A poor mark on a piece of school work can seem disastrous, an argument with a friend can feel as if one's whole life is ruined. The brain has a lot to do with these sensations. The area in the front of the brain, which helps to keep things in proportion, is developing more slowly than the area to do with feelings and emotions. So it is for this reason that there are times when young people feel overwhelmed with feelings (wonder, happiness, disaster, catastrophe, etc.). The bit of the brain that can help the individual see a broader picture is still catching up.

Lastly, and closely related to this, is the ability to think and plan ahead. To be able to do this, the young person also needs the thinking part of the brain to be working well. Of course there will be times when teenagers can manage this perfectly well. However, there may be times when it is more difficult. These will be the times when the prefrontal cortex lags behind the amygdala. Powerful hormones will push for a quick reward. The area of the brain that says: "Hang on a minute, is that wise?" may not be working as well as the area that says "Let's do it, that sounds like fun".

The phrase: "Hang on a minute, is that wise?" may sound like a boring parent talking. We have to be clear that it is fine for the teenager to want to have fun. Indeed, you could say that this stage of life is exactly the time that young people can have fun. Many young people have said to me that when you have a job and have to worry about a mortgage, life cannot be fun anymore. "I guess young people are more interested in having fun whilst they are growing up, but adults have to work and get money for the family, and stuff like that."

The point here is that during these years the teenage brain is helping the individual move forward and become more mature. However, because so much is changing in the brain there will be times when it becomes difficult to manage feelings or to see the wider picture. This is not necessarily a problem. The purpose of this book is to help you understand all aspects of brain development. In some ways, the changes in the teenage brain are hugely helpful and exciting. In other ways, these changes mean that it can be a bit bumpy for a while. This is all part of growing up. It is symbolic of the transition that all young people go through as they move gradually towards being an adult.

Adults can encourage healthy brain development

I have emphasised the fact that the environment around the teenager makes a difference. This is especially true during a critical period of development. Of course the most important aspect of the environment is the home. The home has by far and away the greatest influence on the young person's development. I shall be saying more about this in Chapter 4, where I discuss the significance of adults.

However, while I am considering the development of the brain, it is worth noting some of the things adults can do in this context. Here are four things that adults can do which will have a positive impact on brain development.

• Understanding.
  If adults can make allowances for the fact that teenagers are experiencing a major upheaval and readjustment of their brains, this will make relationships easier and contribute to well-being.
• Hormone balance.
  A good balance of hormones is essential if the brain is to manage the process of pruning unwanted connections, while developing and cementing useful neural pathways. If the young person experiences too much anxiety or stress, the hormone balance will hinder this fundamental process. There is no way to avoid some degree of anxiety and stress, but adults can do all they can to keep this to a reasonable level. In addition, they can help young people learn to manage these difficult emotions.
• The amygdala and the prefrontal cortex.
  The more adults can do to encourage the development of the prefrontal cortex, the better for emotion regulation. The more enriching the environment, and the wider range of activities in which the young person is engaged, the more opportunities there will be for the prefrontal cortex to mature faster.
• Good routines.
  For teenagers routines make a difference. Where sleep is concerned, the melatonin effect can be overcome, but only with good sleep routines. This is hard to manage on your own, so adult help can make a significant difference.

3

THE STAGE FRAMEWORK

Everything that I have said so far underlines the point that the teenage years are a stage of development. The maturation of the brain underpins this process. I have discussed some of the major changes in the brain, and shown how these might affect the way the teenager thinks and behaves. In this chapter I will look at change from a slightly different angle. I want to explore in more detail what the idea of a stage means. I want to illustrate some other aspects of growing up, and indicate how these link with brain development. I also want to propose a framework, which I call the STAGE framework, to help parents and carers make sense of the teenage years.

As I have said, growing up through the teenage years is a process. During this process the individual will constantly be developing and moving towards maturity. At this time the young person will experience a number of major changes that are quite unlike any that have occurred during childhood. I have already discussed the changing brain, and here I will be outlining some of the other main changes that take place during the teenage years.

I liked what one father said, when he described his teenage son as "a work in progress". This is how he described his experience.

> At the end of the day you're just glad they've got their health, and they're not staying out all night, or staying away from school. Of course we've got issues with him being untidy at home, and not doing things you ask. Some of it is quite wearing. But my son is 15 now, and he is calming down. He's not the most communicative, and he can make us pretty angry at times, but you're bound to have these highs and lows. But I'm hoping ..., and I'm reassured, after all it's a work in progress, isn't it? Everyone tells me they come out

the other side, and you can already see it happening. He's changing so fast. It's a stage, isn't it?

Some people believe that the use of the word "stage" is insulting to teenagers. If an adult responds to some aspect of teenage behaviour by saying: "Oh, it's only a stage you're going through", the young person feels patronised, as if their experiences are not really important. The Northumberland Health Authority once published a book about young people's health with the title: *It's not just a phase we're going through*.

This is important. We need to be careful and thoughtful when describing the teenage years as a stage. It is the use of the word "only" that represents the flashpoint. This implies that the young person's experiences do not have any significance, or that they do not need to be taken seriously. Of course this is not the case. In any event for many young people quite the opposite is true. Being able to understand that moods and feelings are transient rather than permanent can be reassuring, as this 15-year-old girl explains.

> I do get moody, I think everyone does at some point. I remember getting very upset about it, and thinking: "Is this it?" sort of thing. Am I just going to be like this, day after day, live my life like this? And my Mum talked to me, and she told me, like, that everything was transient, and that every mood that I had was going to go away eventually, and so you could be right down, but, you know, eventually it will go, and you'll be back up. It's a bit like "I'm growing up!" And it never seemed like such a big thing anymore. But yes, there was a point before I realised that, I just felt like, I'm going to be miserable forever, and my life is always going to be in this system, going to school, or work, or whatever, and it's never going to end.

Here are some of the major changes that make the teenage years distinctive.

- In the first place, these years are a **transition** from childhood to adulthood, and there are particular things about transitions that make them special.
- Second, the beginning of this stage is marked not just by changes in the brain, but by **puberty**, a remarkable and unique process of physical and emotional maturation.

- Interestingly, there is **no clearly defined beginning or end** of the stage of adolescence in our society, and that too has an impact on young people and on the adults around them.
- Finally, the teenage years are characterised by **particular behaviours** which are different from those seen in other stages of life.

I will now describe each of these aspects of the teenage years.

Transition

One mother describes her son as difficult, inconsistent, yet also needing love and affection. The interviewer asks why she thinks teenagers are inconsistent.

> Probably because they're going through the transition from childhood to adulthood. One week they're feeling vulnerable and tend to be more childish, and another they're more confident and trying to assert themselves. You get the pendulum swinging from one to the other. That is sometimes very difficult to cope with.

The transition from child to adult means that the young person is never quite sure where he or she stands. Transitions mean that:

- You are neither one thing nor the other.
- You are impatient to get to the next stage.
- You are excited by new opportunities.
- You are fearful about the unknown future.
- You worry about losing the safety of what is familiar.
- You are confused by new emotions and new experiences.

Every adult who knows teenagers will be familiar with the "flip-flop" of behaviour that is such a feature of these years. As one parent put it: "You never know where you stand. One moment they're up, the next they're down". This changeable behaviour is hard to live with, yet there is a good reason for it. In essence, inside every teenager there is both a child and an adult. During the transition both these aspects of the individual will be expressed at different times. If you can recognise this, it will help you show a little more patience in the face of the inconsistency.

Of course, the brain has a part to play too. You could think about the prefrontal cortex as the "adult" area of the brain – the command

and control centre, while the amygdala is the "child" – the needy and emotional part of the brain. These two sites do not mature at exactly the same rate, so there will be times when one is dominant over the other. This may be a further reason underlying the "flip-flop" of feelings and behaviour.

I will just say a word about being "neither one thing nor the other". This state of uncertainty poses special problems for both the young person and for the adult. Everyone wants to feel comfortable in their role. People want to know where they stand, and what is expected of them. This is true in the family as much as it is in schools and work places. Yet during the process of transition this is not possible. Parents and carers are never quite sure how to treat a teenager during these years of development.

It is difficult for the adult to determine quite how much to expect of a young person, and how much freedom to allow. Yet, for the teenager, this is tricky too. What is reasonable to expect from the parent or carer? On the one hand, the teenager wants to be treated as a responsible person, but sometimes that can be scary. Being looked after and having things done for you can feel safe and comforting. When the young person's behaviour is looked at in this light, it is not difficult to understand the swinging of the pendulum. If these situations are to be managed, nothing is more powerful than open communication, and being able to listen to each other. Being "in transition" is never easy.

Puberty

When most people talk about puberty they think of a girl starting her periods, or a boy whose voice has just broken. These are the outward signs of a major process of change within the body that usually takes place somewhere between the ages of nine and 14. Puberty is the time of the second biggest change in human development. The only time when there is a larger scale of change in the human body is during the first year of life.

It is important to note that puberty involves a lot more than a girl's periods or changes in a boy's voice. Puberty is not only about sexual maturation, or about external body features such as breast development or the arrival of new body hair. Puberty involves changes in the brain and in the hormone balance in the body. It involves changes in blood composition, in muscle growth, and in the major organs of the body such as the lungs and the heart. Puberty also involves a growth spurt, when the individual grows more rapidly than at any time apart from the first 12 months after birth.

Here are some facts about puberty:

- The beginning of puberty is triggered primarily by the release of sex hormones – testosterone in the case of boys and oestrogen in the case of girls.
- All the different changes associated with puberty will last about two years.
- Puberty starts a year or 18 months earlier in girls than in boys.
- There is wide individual variation in the age of puberty and in the sequence of changes. This is perfectly normal.
- The average age for a girl to start her periods at present in the UK is 11 years, 10 months.
- However, approximately one in five girls will have started their periods while still in primary school.
- Although the physical changes will be the obvious ones that can be seen by the outside world, there are also emotional changes going on that are not so obvious.

I should emphasise that there are wide individual differences in the age at which young people experience puberty. Some can start as early as nine or 10, others may not start till 12 or 13. All this is perfectly normal. However, in this sensitive stage no one wants to be "different". Being in step, and not standing out from the crowd, is a very important consideration. As a result many young people, and parents too, get worried about the pace of change. Some worry that nothing is happening, while others worry about whether things are normal or not. Here is one mother's experience.

> I remember my daughter saying "I've got these lumps, I've got these lumps" you know, and it was like "Oh well don't worry, it's breasts starting to grow". And then it was "But it hurts", so then you find out that it's quite normal, and they don't always grow at the same rate, and she's reassured. I think we went through quite a few phases of things not being unexpected, but not being quite how you might have expected them to be, not necessarily all that straightforward, and sort of minor panics. Usually I would say "Don't worry, I'm sure it's perfectly normal", but you know they're bound to worry.

Parents and carers should be sure that they are as fully informed as possible about puberty. This will enable them to offer support and reassurance, especially when the young person is fretting over whether their development is normal or not.

There are a few individuals who experience puberty either very early or very late. This can cause great anxiety for the young people who are affected, and of course for the adults as well. There are cases of girls starting puberty at seven or eight, and at the other end of the age range there are those who do not reach puberty till 15 or 16. If you think this could be the case in your family, then do consult a doctor.

It is really important for parents and carers to know that none of these experiences need have lasting effects. What is critical is that adults know about the possible risks, and provide the necessary information and support for the young person. If the school is not aware of the situation, then the parent should be sure that teachers are informed, so that they too can offer support as appropriate. I should stress that it is unusual for a boy or girl to be so far outside the normal range of experience; however, it does happen, so it is as well for parents to be informed about this possibility.

Research has shown that boys who mature very early usually do well, as they are stronger, taller, and more developed than their peers. This often means that they are good at sport, something that is associated with popularity. On the other hand, boys who mature very much later than others are not necessarily particularly popular, and do not do so well at their school work.

As far as girls are concerned, both early and late development can be problematic. Early puberty may lead to early sexual activity, and thus to relationships with older boys. Later development can have much the same impact as in boys, sometimes leading to poorer social relationships and poorer school attainment.

To conclude this section I want to say a word about the possible psychological effects of puberty on the young person. Here is one girl recalling her emotions around her first period.

> I mean I knew it was going to happen and everything. But I hadn't really prepared for what I was going to feel, the sort of feeling that I've got to go through this every month, blah, blah, blah, and my Mum just sort of said "Yeh, look on it as a gift rather than, sort of, like torture". But I mean to some extent you sort of, well you sort of think "I hate going through this every month, I really hate it.

For parents and carers it is important to recognise that, although the focus will be on the physical changes, there will be a lot of emotional changes going on at the same time. Puberty has an impact on the young person's self-concept, and on their sense of self-worth. Almost everyone worries about whether they are normal or not. There is hardly a teenage boy alive who has not worried about the size of his penis, or a teenage girl who has not worried about the size of her breasts. We know from research that the self-image of girls suffers around puberty, with nearly half of all girls feeling dissatisfied with their bodies.

Even the most confident individual may still feel clumsy and awkward as they adjust to the growth spurt and to new physical sensations. Puberty brings with it such big changes to the body that it is inevitable that there will be a period of adjustment for everyone. There are also some differences between boys and girls here. Because of menstruation it is probably true that girls are better prepared for puberty than boys. As an example, research shows that very few parents talk to their sons about wet dreams.

Puberty can be very straightforward for some, and complicated for others. Some remember it as a time of stress and anxiety, others can hardly recall the changes. What is most important is that adults make sure they understand what is involved, and are therefore able to prepare their daughter or son in the best manner possible. If you want to learn more about puberty do look at the Resources list at the end of the book.

The beginning and the end of the teenage stage

People often ask how long the teenage stage lasts. Not surprisingly parents are keen to know when adolescence begins, and even more importantly, when it ends. There are no easy answers to these questions. As far as the beginning of the stage is concerned, puberty is usually considered the most obvious marker. However, even this is not clear-cut, as puberty can start as early as age nine or 10, or in rare cases even earlier. Some young people may start to show signs of physical development even though they are still very child-like in their emotions. Other teenagers may not start showing signs of puberty till they are 13 or 14. This variation is quite normal.

The best answer is that there is no one change or specific moment that marks the beginning of this stage. It will happen gradually, with various features of adolescence becoming apparent at different times. Parents may notice some elements of "teenage" behaviour appearing before others. Signs of a stroppy attitude, or the wish to make independent decisions, for example, may be early indicators that the young person is beginning to move into a new phase. Girls sometimes show such behaviour earlier than boys. It is not uncommon to hear a parent describe a daughter as "10 going on 16"!

There has been much discussion about whether puberty is starting earlier today than in previous generations. Recent research shows that, over the last 50 years at least, there has not been much change in the age girls start their periods. On the other hand, other signs of physical development are showing changes. For example, girls are starting breast development earlier, and boys' voices are breaking earlier than was the case in the past. Also both boys and girls are taller and heavier than they were even 20 years ago. One of the most likely reasons for this has to do with changes in nutrition.

As far as the end of this stage is concerned, this is even more difficult to define than it is to identify the beginning of adolescence. There is common agreement that it takes longer today to reach adulthood than it did in previous generations. This is because of the major social changes that have taken place, particularly with respect to education and employment.

Interestingly, research on the brain has thrown new light on this topic. We now know that the brain continues to change and mature until the individual is into their mid-20s. This is important, as we often see those in their 20s as fully adult. However, neuroscience has shown us that the brain development continues well past the teenage years.

Here are some of the main social changes that have occurred over the last 20 years:

- A greater proportion of teenagers are staying on longer in secondary education.
- Fewer teenagers are in full-time employment.
- There are fewer long-term job opportunities for young people.
- The types of jobs have changed, with fewer openings in manufacturing and more opportunities in the service industries.
- More young people continue into higher education, with nearly 50% in the UK going to college or university.
- Housing for young people is very hard to find. As a result most remain at home, or return home after college.
- The age of leaving home has steadily increased over the past 20 years.

These facts have a major impact on the lives of young people, and on the way they achieve adulthood. Most remain financially dependent on their parents, and many live under the same roof. This can lead to resentment and conflict. Even in the best of circumstances, there needs to be a lot of give and take between the generations for this stage to work well for all the family.

Most important of all, this situation means that it is very difficult for an individual young person to know when she, or he, can be considered grown up. How can this be defined? Even more difficult, what exactly does "grown up" mean in our world today?

Most young people cannot be fully independent from their parents for many years. Clearly, therefore, financial independence is not much use for determining when someone has reached the end of this stage. As a result young men and young women turn to other markers, such as having freedom to determine their own leisure activities, friendships, sexual behaviour, or drug and alcohol use.

All this means that it is harder than ever to be sure when this stage comes to an end. This can pose problems for parents, and for young adults too.

- For how long should parents go on giving a helping hand?
- Should parents expect their son or daughter to pay rent?
- When should parents give advice, and when keep silent?
- What happens when the two generations have a major disagreement?
- How does the family manage if the young woman or young man wants to have a partner living at home?

The point at which this stage can be said to come to an end is far from clear. Every individual will experience the process of moving to adulthood in a slightly different way. For parents, it is clearly important to recognise the effect that this has on the young adult. The lack of clarity can lead to uncertainty and confusion. Families will need to work together to tackle the challenges. Open communication between the generations will be necessary if young adults are to move into adulthood without too much stress.

Behaviours associated with the teenage years

To end this chapter I will refer briefly to some of the behaviours that mark this stage out as different from other stages. Many of the parents who were interviewed for this book were able to give graphic descriptions of behaviours that defined the teenage years. One good example of this is when the teenager gets annoyed with the parent, just for existing. One mother told us that her daughter became irritated when she coughed, or even cleared her throat. Here is a father describing the same reaction:

> One of the things I've noticed is that they are less tolerant of you, they become more aware of you as a person, they're more critical of you. So it's things like "Oh Dad, do you have to do that?" Particularly at dinner, they'll be critical of my eating habits, for example "Can you not do that? Can you not scrape your fork on your plate like that?" And, "do you have to breathe so heavily?" is the other one I get. "But I'm just breathing." "Yeah, but don't breathe like that." "Like what?" "In the way that you are!" Things like that start to creep in, and there's been the odd occasion when she's said "I can't sit here, I just can't," and she'll go stomping off because I'm breathing when I'm eating. And you start to question yourself a bit, am I really turning into this old git?

Another feature of behaviour during these years is that young people give the impression of being very self-centred. Their world is the only world, and they appear to live very much for the moment. In the previous chapter I mentioned the intense preoccupation with the self that arises as a result of changes in the brain. The individual, especially in early adolescence, becomes painfully aware of how she or he appears to other people. As a result there will be times when behaviour will seem to be immature, and what is known as "adolescent egocentrism" may be one reflection of this.

Many parents commented on this. Here are two parents describing their experiences:

> It's like a train on a track, and I think when they get to 14/15 it's like they've gone into a tunnel and the only thing they see at the end of that very very long tunnel is a reflection of themselves, and you're in the pitch darkness, you're not in their field of vision at all.

> Remembering back, I know you become so self-absorbed. I know I was the classic teenager, moody, wearing black, completely self-absorbed, and you think this is your whole world, and it will never change. It's really difficult to think outside of yourself and your time at that point. You think this is how it will be like forever, it's never going to change.

The need for privacy is also a feature of this stage. Someone once described this to me as follows. The teenager is like an actor in the dressing room. They are trying on different costumes, worrying about how they will look to the audience, and they have a period when they are not ready to come out on to the stage. The need for privacy during these years is a reflection of the state of uncertainty and confusion in early adolescence.

> I wouldn't say my son is particularly secretive, but he's not as forthcoming. He likes to keep his bedroom locked. It's very important to him to keep his privacy at all costs. I fought against that at first, but I've accepted it now. This is an area where I'm cut off. It's a bit strange, as it's a bit of the house that is cut off from all of us. It's his territory.

One last example of behaviour that is symbolic of the teenage years relates to the changeable nature of moods and relationships. I have already mentioned this in the context of the changing brain, and in relation to transition. I have described the flip-flop of emotions that is so common at this stage. I come back to it here as this often seems to be one of the central features of teenage behaviour. Many parents talked about their experiences. Here is one mother's description of her daughter's behaviour.

> I suppose my emotions are a little bit confused, because you can say something to her, one day she'll take it the right way, then next day it will be completely the wrong way. You have to think every time "what am I going to say to her?" You don't know how she's going to react. It's just mood swings, isn't it? The thing is with my daughter if something is not right in her little world with friends and whatever then she's horrible, but if everything is right she can be quite sweet. It's difficult to read the situation, because you don't know what's going on. I suppose it's another world going on out there, isn't it?

I can only emphasise that all these behaviours have their place. They are not necessarily comfortable for the young person, or of course for you as a parent. These behaviours are not designed to get at you, or to hurt you, or to push you away. They are a way of dealing with the pressures and demands of a maturing process.

It may also be helpful to keep in mind that change does not happen overnight. It can sometimes feel as if no change is happening at all. The teenage years are a very long stage, and much of the change will be slow or invisible. Understanding that this is a stage and a process of gradual change will help you understand your teenager. As I noted in the first chapter, another reason for using the word STAGE to describe the framework I am proposing is that each letter of the word represents a key element of parenting. I will now turn to an examination of each of these elements, starting with the letter S for significance.

4

S – THE SIGNIFICANCE OF PARENTS AND CARERS

S – Significance
T – Two-way communication
A – Authority
G – Generation gap
E – Emotion

In the following chapters I will discuss the five key elements that are associated with each of the letters in the word STAGE. To begin with I will discuss S – the idea of significance – showing why parents of teenagers are so very important. This is a point I have made already in describing brain development. The brain and the environment develop hand in hand. Each influences the other. Enriching and supportive home environments encourage healthy brain development. It follows that parents have a key part to play here. Yet there is still a lot of confusion about the role of parents during the teenage years.

The views of parents

One of the most common views of parents is the belief that they are not important any more. In the interviews we carried out parent after parent talked about their sense that they no longer mattered very much. They felt that friends and the peer group had, in some way, taken over.

In these situations parents feel that friends have become more influential and important to the teenager than the parents themselves. This is a difficult emotion to manage, as it is associated with feeling powerless, and with losing control over your own children. Even when parents recognise that this has not happened yet, they still fear that it will occur soon. Here is a mother with one daughter, and then a father with two sons.

One of my fears is that I will not be important any more – that peer relations become more important and there's a sort of transference of talking to, which goes from me to her peers, so she will no longer talk about personal things which she has done up to now. And that I'll lose a sense of feeling close to her, in knowing her quite intimately....

Yes, probably I am too emotional, because I wanted what I felt was right for them. To be defied quite a lot I found very hard to accept.... The influence of other teenagers I found the biggest problem. They had greater influence on my sons than I did. I admit I did get very angry at times about that.

In the STAGE framework the "S" stands for significance. The "S" represents the fact that parents of teenagers matter just as much as parents of younger children, it is just that they matter in a different way. So how can this be explained if the experiences of parents appear to reflect the opposite?

The evidence

Let us consider the evidence. All the research we have on parenting tells us how important parents are during these years. Where teenagers manage well, it is usually because their parents have been there for them. This does not mean simply giving them money or material goods. It does mean showing an interest, and being there to provide support at key moments.

I will take one good example. Studies of school achievement show that, apart from actual intelligence, the factor that makes the most difference to a teenager's success at school is parental interest and involvement. If the parents are engaged with the teenager's learning, and show that this is important to them, this will provide a powerful incentive for the young person. Of course this does not mean going up to the school all the time, and badgering the teachers. But it does mean taking an interest in homework. It means being concerned about how the young person is getting on, and being supportive if things are not going well.

It would be wrong to claim that this works all the time. There are, of course, situations where relationships between parent and teenager are not good. In such situations the young person may reject the parents' concern and interest. I will have more to say about such situations later in the book. However, broadly speaking, parents do matter. Parents are role models, and they play a key role in many different areas. They will be influential where the young person's health is concerned, they will have an impact on attitudes and values, and they will shape many aspects of behaviour. Most importantly, the way the two parents relate to each other will have a huge impact on the teenager's ideas about couples and about how two people can share a task as important as parenting

Negative identity

As they move through the teenage years young people seek to be independent of adults. This means not accepting the rules set by parents, and expressing opinions which are different from those of adults. A well-known psychoanalyst and writer on adolescence, Erik Ericson, describes this stage as one of *negative identity*.

In this stage the teenager wants to be different. He or she may not know what they want, or who they are, but they do know one thing. They want to be the exact opposite of what their parents want. They are not going to do the things their parents expect, or become the sort of person their parents want them to become! Hence the notion of *negative identity*.

Independence

The search for independence creates challenges for adults. It is hard to be told that you are out of date, or that you simply don't understand! It is also hard to learn that your son or daughter prefers to listen to their friends rather than to you. Yet, this is an important process for young people. They need to be able to try out new ideas, and experiment with taking control of their own lives. Unless they have the chance to do this, they cannot grow up and become mature adults. As one father said:

> It's so hard when they start questioning your decisions, and what you regard as your wisdom. There are times when it is difficult to be able to cross the barrier between what you think or know is right, and what they want to do. They think you're just being awkward or stubborn, and not moving with the times.

A lot of this has to do with power in the family. Who has control? Who makes the decisions? Since the children were toddlers parents have, by and large, been able to control the situation. Perhaps children have made small decisions, about friends or clothes for example, but in the main parents have held the reins. Mothers and fathers have been able to feel that, when it comes to the important things, their wishes will carry the day.

This situation changes, however, with the arrival of the teenage years. Gradually the power balance in the family shifts, and young people begin to claim power for themselves. They do this in many different ways: through direct disagreement and argument, by becoming more private, or by turning to their friends.

It is this shift in power that some parents find hard to manage. And it is this which can lead to the sense that parents don't matter anymore. Here is one mother talking about her feelings.

It's complete and utter frustration at times, and it's upsetting too when they cut you off. And you think: "I'm only trying to do positive things here, I'm only trying to do good". And you think: "Why don't you want this? It's here, you don't have to do it all on your own". There's been times when I've been so frustrated I've just wanted to walk away. But in the end you know they have to go through it, don't they?

Parents do matter

In spite of all this, parents do matter. Someone once said that, for teenagers, the family is like the wallpaper. You only notice it when the paper is peeling away, or when you want to change the colour. In other words most of the time parents are the backdrop, rather than the central feature in the young person's landscape. Nonetheless this should not be confused with the idea that parents do not matter. If parents are not there, or if parents are not providing support, you can be sure the young person will be only too well aware of this.

A friend of mine said teenagers are a bit like the terrible twos. They actually need the same amount of time and attention. And I kind of thought: "What's he talking about?" But I had it in my mind, and I realise it makes sense. We tend to think "Oh! They're teenagers". Because their attitude is often a matter of go away, close the door, I want to do my own stuff. But actually if you provide areas of contact they do want that interaction, and they need it as much as in a way the equivalent of what I call the twos and threes.

Parents matter because they provide, among other things:

- warmth, nurturance, and love,
- stability,
- support in times of difficulty,
- confirmation that the young person matters,
- structure and boundaries,
- a role model for everything from health behaviours to managing conflict,
- a supportive environment for healthy brain development.

Even if it appears that your son or daughter's friends matter more, this is only part of a particular stage of development. In this stage it is necessary for the teenager to show independence and to be separate from the parents. Remember what I said about *"negative identity"*? In spite of this, there are a myriad hidden ways in which parents will be playing a key role. Patterns of communication, and the way authority is exercised, are two prime examples of ways in which the behaviour of parents makes a difference to the young person. I will be dealing with these topics in the next two chapters.

There are a number of messages I hope you will take from this book. One of the most important is that parents matter! Parents of teenagers are significant!

5

T – TWO-WAY
COMMUNICATION

S – Significance
T – Two-way communication
A – Authority
G – Generation gap
E – Emotion

The T in STAGE stands for two-way communication. Not all communication is two-way. Indeed teenagers often say that their parents are either interrogating them or telling them to do certain things such as their homework. This can be described as one-way communication. One person does the talking. This is very different from a situation where there is as much listening as talking. Here we call this two-way communication because each individual has the chance to talk and can feel that they are being listened to. I believe this is a critical aspect of the contact between adults and teenagers. Talking is at the core of relationships in the family. Yet for many parents this seems to be one of the biggest hurdles of all.

One of the questions often asked at workshops for parents of teenagers is: "How can I get my son (or daughter) to talk to me"? Parents wish that they could talk easily to their teenager. They want to be able to communicate, but very often the young person does not seem interested. Why is this? What lies behind the silence, the grunting, or the arguments?

As I have already noted, the shift in the balance of power is directly relevant here. One of the ways that teenagers express their independence is by taking a more active role in communication.

This can be seen in many different ways:

• the teenager only wants to talk at certain times,
• the teenager does not want to talk at all,

- the teenager gets cross at being questioned,
- the teenager feels she (or he) is not being listened to,
- the teenager clams up because the adult "does not understand",
- the teenager wants to argue rather than to listen.

One of the strands running through recent research on adolescents and the family has to do with the fact that relationships always go two ways. Earlier in the book I mentioned research on "information management", which has highlighted how young people manage what they tell their parents and what they hold back.

Adults may think they are doing the talking, or making the decisions. Parents may think that communication is going one way – from the parent to the teenager. In fact communication goes both ways, with the young person taking as much control as the parent.

As an illustration of this, here is one father's frustrating experience with his teenagers.

> I think they get what would seem to be like negative attention. You're telling them off because, you know, you've already told them five times before, but they're still getting that attention, and they've got you focussed on them, and it plays on your emotions probably more than on theirs. Because to them you're wrong, you know nothing, you don't understand, you're my parent, and so they're not listening. Whereas I think: why have I not been able to hold the conversation, argue this point, get them to see my way and get an outcome?

Clearly such experiences are not helpful for either adult or young person. In this chapter I will be exploring how things can go wrong, and what can be done about it.

Communication is a two-way street

As I noted earlier communication is a two-way street. Yet almost everyone makes the assumption that if they are talking the other person will be listening. This may not be the case, as is well illustrated in the quote above. In many situations teenagers do not pay attention to everything that is said. They may only hear half the words that are spoken. A key point here is that people are far more likely to listen if they think the other person is also listening to them. This is an important factor in communication between a parent and young person.

Teenagers often say that the parent only wants to talk at them, but does not listen to their point of view. However, talking and listening go hand in hand. In a conversation where there is a relatively equal distribution of talking and listening communication usually works well. When one person does most of the talking, then exactly the opposite is the case. If parents and teenagers are to communicate well, then there has to be as much listening as talking.

Here is a parent who is struggling with how best to communicate with a teenager. This father is still thinking about communication as getting his son or daughter to accept his point of view.

A lot of people say that teenagers feel parents are talking at them and not to them. Parents tend to say "The facts are these", and that turns out to be talking at them. I find you need to be exceptionally clever to lead your children into accepting something. It's so difficult not to ask questions, and teenagers don't like questions. They think it's an interrogation!

This emphasises the importance of thinking about the listener as much as thinking about what you are saying. A consideration here is that the words that come out of our mouths are only a small part of the total communication package. You might think that what you have said is quite clear, but what is happening to the listener can get in the way and influence what is actually heard. The listener may be thinking of something else, and only hear half of what you say. They may misinterpret your tone of voice. They may already have switched off before you open your mouth.

One good piece of advice therefore when you want to communicate is to think as much about the listener as about yourself and what you want to say. Try to put yourself in the position of the listener. What is happening to them while you are talking? This will help you tailor the message to suit the situation, and increase the chances that you will be heard.

Filters and information management

Continuing on this theme, it is helpful to think of the listener operating a series of filters. These filters modify the message that is being communicated. One filter that plays an important part where teenagers are concerned is the filter of the power relationship. To take one example, the simple question from a parent: "How are you getting on with your homework?" can be filtered by the teenager into: "I am telling you, because I am your parent, to get on with your homework!". Now of course this is not what the parent actually says, but this is what the message becomes once it has gone through the filter of "My parent is trying to show that she/he has power over me".

Here is a good example of a parent who has not thought about the power filter.

> I don't know if my children find it hard to communicate with me, or if it wouldn't be more honest to say they don't really wish to communicate with me terribly! I don't feel I have difficulty in communicating with them, I just have difficulty in stopping them for 5 minutes to be prepared to listen to me while I communicate with them as they are not terribly interested. I get them in a corner and say: "Will you listen to this because I consider that it is very important".

Another filter that often operates with teenagers is that of expectation. If someone expects a message on a certain topic, this is what they will hear, even though it was not intended in that way. A girl who expects her mother to nag her about her untidy bedroom will hear that message, even though the mother may want to talk about something quite different.

This is a good moment to bring in the topic of information management. This is also a filter, but it is a filter used by the speaker rather than by the listener. This is something we all do. We all choose to tell members of our family some things, and to hold back others. Indeed life would be impossible if we had to tell everyone everything that happens to us. However, the important point about the research on teenagers is that it has enabled us to learn a lot more on how young people make decisions about what to tell their parents.

This research shows that:

- Teenagers think very carefully about how to manage information.
- Teenagers make their decisions on what to talk about based on all sorts of reasons, some of which are about protecting their parents, or not wanting to worry them.
- Teenagers have clear and well thought-out views about what parents ought to know, and what things they do not need to know.
- Research on information management is one of the best examples of why communication is a two-way process.

Communication is a skill

While we realise that such things as driving a car, or cooking, involve the development of a skill, it is rarely recognised that communication is a skill too. This is a good time to link what I am saying here with earlier information about brain development. Because of the development of the prefrontal cortex, teenagers go through a time of rapid change in their thinking and language development. Learning to communicate is part of this process of development.

An increase in vocabulary is another reflection of the maturation of the language areas of the brain. It may be of interest to note that the vocabulary of an average 14- or 15-year-old contains only about 75% of the words in an adult vocabulary. Think about how difficult it would be for you to talk about a strong emotion if you only had three-quarters of the words that you normally use!

Teenagers often say that adults are "good at it". In other words, to them it looks as if adults are able to find the right words and explain themselves easily. Teenagers, on the other hand, struggle to find the right words. They feel they are not very good at explaining themselves. This is one of the reasons that young people hold back, or remain silent. They are not as confident as adults, and not unnaturally they do not want to look silly. Communication is a skill, and it has to be learnt. Parents can play a big role here in understanding this, and helping young people develop this skill.

Communication is more than talking

As readers will be aware, communication is not just talking. An enormous amount can be communicated through gestures, tone of voice, eye-contact, the way you stand, and so on. This is often called non-verbal communication. All these things convey just as powerful a message as the actual words that are used. You can use very reasonable words, yet by your non-verbal communication you can make it clear that you are very angry. Take the words "I am listening to you". You may want to try and say these words in a number of different ways. You will find that even a slightly different emphasis on a word gives a different meaning to the sentence! It is surprising how much can be conveyed through tone of voice.

One important aspect of non-verbal communication with teenagers has to do with timing. Most parents know that there are good and bad times to tackle a tricky subject with a teenager. Of course this is true of all communication, but because of the issues we have

41

been discussing, timing is especially important in this context. It makes sense to find a time that best suits the teenager if you want to talk about something important. As all parents will know, teenagers often choose precisely the least convenient time, such as late at night, to open their hearts. Yet seizing the moment can pay large dividends. You may hear things that would never come out at any other time.

How emotion affects communication

So far in this chapter I have been taking a very rational approach to communication. However, none of us can be rational all the time. Often emotions get in the way, especially with teenagers. It is important to recognise that feelings, such as tiredness, irritation, or frustration, can play a big role in affecting communication. Here is one good example.

> I have found it difficult to communicate with my daughter at times. For me, it's to do with not being listened to, and not listening. Me being caught up in my own world. I get back from work, and I'm tired, I've been giving out all day, and I actually need a break and some time for me, and she may not be sensitive to that. It's the same the other way around – that I'm not sensitive enough to her needs. At that point communication tends to break down.

Many parents talk of getting frustrated. It can feel as if the teenager will not listen, deliberately ignoring what the parent is saying. This frustration is bound to affect how communication works. The more frustrated someone gets, the harder it is to listen carefully, or to take into account the other person's point of view. In these situations "I" statements can help. I will say more about these in a moment.

It is also the case that in situations where emotions run high, conflict can escalate. Arguments can run and run because of the anger that is behind the words, or things can be said that take a long time to put right again.

> I must say when you do get in an argument with them, and they're saying really nasty stuff, you can say something that to you isn't that bad, but they will take it to heart. In an argument I did once say: "You remind me of your father right now", and it was the worst thing I could have said. It wasn't until he opened up 6 months later that I realised what

a detrimental effect that one sentence had had. So what I say to people is: be careful what negative things come out of your mouth!

While on this subject it is also important to recognise that at times a parent might not want to hear what the teenager has to say. In the best of situations parents will want to listen to the young person. Yet sometimes that is very hard to do. As an example, a mother might know very well that the teenager wants her to be at home after school, but the demands of her job could mean that this is impossible. This then becomes an unspoken tension between them. The young person wants to "complain" about the situation, but the mother does not want to hear. In such circumstances it takes considerable strength on the part of a parent to allow such a discussion.

There is no easy answer to these problems. Awareness of some of the things I have been saying about communication may help. Emotions, particularly negative emotions, can play a very large role in relationships between parents and teenagers. Being able to stand back, take a deep breath, and have a break for a few moments is often the best way to manage in these situations. It is also important to remember that the teenager's feelings of frustration and anger may be more about their own emotional world than about you as a parent. I will have more to say about these things in Chapter 8 when I discuss the E for emotion.

"I" statements

When you are cross or upset with your teenager it is easy to become critical. You may feel that your teenager has behaved badly, or been selfish or careless. In these situations most parents find it hard not to blame the young person. You may find yourself saying: "You drive me mad". "You should have been more careful". "You are just so selfish". "This is all your fault".

People who have long experience in making communication easier have pointed out that placing the blame on the other person is likely to lead to communication breakdown. The other person feels defensive, and stops talking. Or the other person gets even more cross, and the argument escalates.

A different approach is to use "I" statements. Here you are careful to make statements that are limited to stating your own emotions. You are not accusing or blaming, you are simply stating your own feelings. "I feel upset about what has happened". "This situation makes me feel cross/sad/frustrated etc.". You are not talking about the other person, you are talking about yourself. This will allow both you and your teenager to be more open with each other.

You will find that using "I" statements makes it very much easier to keep communication channels open, even if there are strong emotions flying around. If you can own your feelings the other person may be able to do the same, without becoming defensive. It is hard to do at first, but do try. Anyone who has used "I" statements will vouch for the impact they can have on communication.

Some tips to improve communication with your teenager

I will conclude the chapter with a couple of good quotes, which include some helpful tips. First, the quotes

> My daughter comes in, she's got a long face. You can tell by the way she throws her bag down that she's a bit ratty. I don't rush her. I'll let her unwind, and then I'll say: "Come on, I want to talk to you". She'll sit down, relax a bit, and I'll say: "Someone's been having a go at you. Something's been irritating you. Now before I do the dinner let's sit down, unwind, and let's talk". And we'll talk, and I'll make a joke, and she'll start laughing, and she'll get it out of her system. I do this with anyone, my husband, anyone. If they want to talk, ok. If they don't, maybe you ask them in a couple of hours when they're in the mood.

> Communication is something that must be two ways. If you allow them to speak to you, they will listen to you. You won't always understand each other, and there will be conflicts of personality, and there will be huge conflicts of preference at times. But they should know why you want what you want, and vice versa. Communication doesn't necessarily mean agreement. A measure of conflict is probably healthy. Conflict can be good if it's through communication, but if it's through blockage, because of a failure of communication, that's different. You've got to show an ability to change your judgement sometimes otherwise they'll stop telling you things.

Now for the tips

- Timing. This is one of the key things about communication. Your teenager will not always want to talk at the time that is best for you. If you have a busy life, and there are things you want to get off your chest, this can be frustrating. However, if you can wait for the right moment you may find you can have a really good conversation. "If they want to talk, ok. If they don't, maybe you'll ask them in a couple of hours ...".

- Agreement/disagreement. It is important to remember that you do not always have to reach agreement with your teenager. If you are trying to force acceptance of your opinion, you may well run into a brick wall. Accepting differences between you and your teenager means that you recognise the teenager has a valid point of view. "Communication does not necessarily mean agreement".

- Try not to come across as judgemental. Because of the lack of confidence at this stage, it is hard for a teenager to accept being judged. "You've got to show an ability to change your judgement, otherwise they'll stop telling you things."

- Humour. Most people enjoy a joke and a bit of humour. Humour can take the tension out of conflict or disagreement. If you can see the funny side of a difficult situation, your teenager will appreciate that. "I'll make a joke, and she'll start laughing, and she'll get it out of her system."

- Careless words. When people are stressed or furious, they may say things in the heat of the moment that can be upsetting or hurtful. Of course teenagers cannot be protected from the parent's strong feelings. However, during the teenage years young people are especially sensitive. Being mocked, derided, or undermined can be hard to take. As one parent put it: "Be careful what comes out of your mouth".

- Be willing to listen. This is probably the most important tip of all. Communication is a two-way process. The more you are able to listen, and hear what the teenager is saying, the more likely it is that the teenager will be able to hear what you have to say.

6

A – AUTHORITY

S – Significance
T – Two-way communication
A – Authority
G – Generation gap
E – Emotion

The way in which parents exercise authority will have a fundamental impact on family relationships during the teenage years. Yet it is a challenge to be able to do this well. Some parents give up too early, while others try and hold on to their authority for too long. Getting the balance right is never easy, so in this chapter I will explore what teenagers need, and how parents can use their authority wisely.

> I have a friend whose mother is like, really cool. She lets her smoke weed in the house, and stuff like that. She's really nice, you can talk to her, but I wouldn't want her as a Mum. Because it's all a bit random, like she's too much of a mate, and there's no security, rules, and stuff. And I think my friend thinks that too.
>
> (15-year-old girl)

What does this mean? This girl is referring to the teenagers' need for structure and rules. Without these it all feels a bit "random". I want to explore this idea in more detail.

Parenting styles

I am going to start by looking at what are called "parenting styles". These refer to the different ways that parents behave with their teenage daughters or sons. Some parents put more emphasis on discipline, while others are more relaxed and flexible about what the teenager is allowed to do. The research on parenting styles has shown that there is one style that leads to the best outcomes for young people. This style is known as the "authoritative" parenting style, because the parent is warm and loving, but also firm when necessary. The parent who embraces the "authoritative" style also promotes autonomy and independence, graded according to the age and maturity of the individual teenager.

Different parenting styles can lead to more or less conflict. Thus a parent who is strong on discipline may expect to have to deal with more conflict than someone who is indifferent or indulgent. The mother who was described as "cool" in the quote above would be described as having an "indulgent" style. She may have chosen that form of behaviour to avoid conflict. Yet, as is made clear, that is not what most teenagers need.

At the heart of the research on parenting styles lie two dimensions of parenting behaviour. These are:

- responsiveness,
- demandingness.

The parent described as "authoritative" would be high on both these dimensions. Thus an "authoritative" parent would be responsive to the individual needs of the young person, and as I have said, would be warm and loving. However, this parenting style also involves a high level of demandingness. This means having clear expectations, and communicating these to the teenager. It also means providing firm boundaries so that the young person has a structure which offers a safe framework within which to grow up.

> I think the kids who don't have any sort of rules or limitations have a problem – it's scary for them. I can just speak about my experience with the youth club, but there I just saw how kids could get very freaked out by feeling that they have no boundaries, no guidelines, and it's a big fear. And although they may seem as if they don't want it, they are crying out for it, and often seem so relieved when it's set out for them.

Setting boundaries and limits will lead to conflict. However, if this can be done in a way that makes it clear that the parent has the welfare of the young person at heart, rather than the parents' convenience, this will help. It is worth remembering that a clear structure set by parents may not be what the young person appears to want, but without it he or she will be lost.

To summarise then, the most effective way to respond to the teenage years is:

- to be open to the individual needs of the young person,
- to show that the teenager is valued and respected,
- to set firm boundaries,
- to show that the parent has expectations of how the teenager will behave and what they will achieve.

Co-parenting

In talking about parenting styles it is important to keep in mind that there will be two parents involved, and they may not have the same approach to parenting. Indeed it is inevitable that two adults in a parenting role will disagree at times. In some cases it may just be a difference of approach on one issue, while in other families it may be that the two parents have very different styles.

> There is a bad atmosphere in the house, well not all the time obviously, but at times it can be really tense, and with my husband and myself sometimes he maybe says: "Goodness, you know, you're being a bit hard on him". And then I have to stand back and see if I'm being too strict, or something like that. When there's a husband and wife in the house you sort of maybe have two different points of view about a situation and how to deal with it.

Whether two parents are living together or living apart after separation, the way in which they manage the parenting task will have a profound impact on the teenager. Young people will be quick to seize on any differences between parents, and will exploit these if they possibly can.

> They will always try and find any chink in the armour between parents, so my husband and I have to show a united front, and we don't always get that right!

Many parents talk about "singing from the same song sheet", and yet as this mother admits, it can sometimes be very hard to achieve. Parents may genuinely have different views about how to deal with a situation. Alternatively, because of a busy life, they may simply not have the time to plan and work things out together before a situation arises.

There are bound to be differences of opinion between two parents. In the best of circumstances the two adults will have the chance to talk things through and agree a common approach. Where this is not possible the key thing is not to allow the differences to be exploited by the young person. It is best to avoid the possibility that the teenager will be able to say: "Oh! But Dad said I could do this", or "But, Mum allows me to do so and so".

There is no point in pretending to your teenager that you agree on everything, if this is obviously not the case. However, your teenager needs to know two things:

- that you are going to back each other up,
- that you will not allow the teenager to get between you.

Here is one mother's view of how to do the best you can to show both these things to your teenager.

> I think there's something about parenting together. I think the huge thing is that you show unity to the child, no matter how much you scream and yell at each other afterwards, and argue after the fact, you have to show unity. We have a good old argument about it, and then we work out how we'll try and stop that happening the next time, we'll talk about it, you have to talk about it. The lines of communication have to be open with your child, they have to be open with your partner too, because otherwise it's a disaster!

Rules – what are they for?

This is a difficult one, but it links closely with what has already been said. If there are no rules, there is no structure. The young person needs structure to provide a feeling of safety and containment in the home. Of course teenagers will not like rules, as they send a message that the parents are the ones who are in control. Young people will find all sorts of ways to challenge the rules. They may cause aggravation and distress to parents in the process. However, parents must hold firm, and stick to their guns.

It is very important that the rules themselves are sensible. Rules for teenagers should have certain characteristics which will make them easier to enforce.

- First, the rules should be simple to explain, and have a clear rationale.
- If at all possible the rules should be negotiated with the young person, so that they have a say in how these are worked out.
- The rules should be for the benefit of the young person, or for the benefit of the family as a whole.
- Rules should not be set solely for the benefit of the adult.
- Ideally rules should relate to the teenager's safety, welfare, or well-being.
- Rules should not be constructed simply because they fit with the parents' beliefs.
- Lastly, parents should try and have as few rules as possible. The fewer the rules, the easier it will be to ensure that they are upheld.

Here is a summary of one parent's experience of working things out together.

> I discovered quite by accident that, when we were talking about what time they should be home at night, if I said: "What time do you think?" they generally said a time that was earlier than I had expected! I considered this to be a superb way of negotiating! I was surprised how sensible they were. Of course if they said: "3 o'clock in the morning" I would say: "That's ridiculous", and then they would laugh and say "OK! I suppose so. Let's get real!".

What to do if the rules are broken?

The rules will be broken, so that is something that has to be accepted. However, if they are sensible rules, then it will be possible for the parent to point out the consequences of breaking them. It should also be possible to show that they are there for the benefit of the young person. Being overly punitive is not helpful. This will only encourage the young person to become more challenging and more distant.

It is equally important that the teenager does learn that there will be consequences when rules are broken. Otherwise what is the point of having them? The teenager may kick up a fuss about any consequences, but the parent should hold firm. Often it is surprising how the young person will, once he or she has calmed down, accept a parent's firm control. This is illustrated nicely in the following example.

In things that concern their welfare they should have a lot of say, but I do think there are some decisions that parents have to make and stick to them. I found this when my daughter was 16 and wanting to go to parties and things. A lot of her friends did go, and she started stretching me to see how many parties she could go to. One week she had three things organised, and I put my foot down. I said: "You can't cope with this and college". So we had terrible dramas. "You're ruining my life, you won't let me do anything interesting, I'm a prisoner here". She was getting really dramatic, so I said she could go to one, but she wouldn't choose. So I said: "That's it, you go to none". She didn't go out at all, and for a fortnight she was quite calm. I think she needed someone strong behind her to do that. There are times when you have to stick to your guns and prepare for the dramas and accusations. Afterwards I think she realised she was being unreasonable.

Sanctions for teenagers

Sanctions for teenagers will need to be different from those used with younger children. They will need to be age-appropriate, and relevant to the teenager's situation. One parent said to me: "What is the point of grounding him when we live on a busy road and he hardly ever goes out anyway?". Sanctions used most often by parents of teenagers include grounding (where appropriate), loss of privileges, loss of pocket money, confiscating devices such as laptops, gaming machines, and I-Pads, and setting various restrictions on freedom.

I have to stress that there are times when none of these things work, as this parent explains.

I think she's too old to ground now, she's 15 and a half, and she thinks she's too old. It's almost quite silly to say: "Look, you're grounded" when she'd be off. It's like: "Oh, is that all you can do?" She has her own key, she's got her phone, she's got a bus pass. There's no point in grounding her because she'll always go out anyway. You can't keep a kid locked up, and sometimes I think it is better that she is out with her friends, and she does calm down you know! And the funny thing is if we have had an argument, 10 minutes later she'll text me, and she's talking as though nothing has happened. It's very strange, it really is very strange! It's just like – back to normal now!

One of the lessons of this example is that sanctions have to be age-appropriate. Grounding is fine for younger teenagers, but not for those who are 15 and a half! It may also be the case that sanctions become less useful or relevant as the teenager becomes older. As this mother says, her daughter already has so much independence that there's not much the mother can do. Once the young person reaches this stage, then rules will be a matter of negotiation rather than imposition.

There are no right or wrong answers here, as each family will have different ideas about what will work with their particular teenager. Once again it is worth noting that harsh or overly punitive sanctions are almost always counter-productive. Finally, if the rationale for the use of a particular sanction can be explained to the teenager, this will make it just that bit more likely that some useful learning can take place.

Types of disobedience

There are many ways that teenagers can be disobedient. These may not always involve direct confrontation, but can include disrespectful behaviour, lying and secrecy, pretence of not having understood the rules, temper tantrums, and obstructive behaviour. Every parent will have their own story of how their daughter or son finds ways of getting round the rules. Everyone will know teenagers who spin stories about the last bus being cancelled, the phone not working, or having to stay late at a party to look after a sick friend. Once again it is worth emphasising that the more sensible the rules, the less likely it will be that the parent has to deal with flagrant disobedience.

It is important to say that there will be some families for whom the suggestions I have outlined here simply do not work. There are young people who do not respond to an approach which involves talking and negotiating. There are some teenagers who treat sanctions as if they are nothing but a nuisance, and do not appear to learn or to engage in sensible discussion. Young people who stay out very late at night, who use drugs, or who get involved with an anti-social peer group will require a different approach.

I do not pretend that there are any simple answers as to how to deal with these situations. Each is unique in its own way. In Chapter 14 I will be discussing what parents can do when things go badly wrong during the teenage years. For the moment I will just say that there will be some teenagers who, for whatever reason, lose that essential connection with their parents which makes the setting of reasonable boundaries possible. While these young people may be in a very small minority, they represent a big challenge to parents and to other adults.

It was clear from the interviews that when a teenager is being difficult parents can feel as if things have spun out of control. This is a very uncomfortable place to be.

I've got a sister-in-law who's been having terrible trouble with her teenage daughter. She didn't know where she was. She knew she was at an all-night party. I said: "Why didn't you ask her where she was going?". The reaction was: "No, I couldn't do that because it would be spying". I said: "She's walking all over you! You've got to stand up to her". And my sister-in-law said she couldn't do that.

When the boundaries are too loosely defined the teenagers appear to be just out of order a lot of the time. The parents end up not quite knowing how to respond, and feeling quite lost, and also humiliated I suppose. I can think of a situation where a parent I know is often being insulted, and she doesn't know how to react to it. I think the teenager on the one hand actually needs someone to say you're out of order, but the parent is not sure enough of herself to say you're out of order.

It is very hard for parents to feel that things are out of control. It can lead to feelings of intense anger and frustration, or it can make parents sad and depressed. It is also often the case that this situation creates bad feeling between the two parents, with each blaming the other for the situation.

Many of the things I have discussed in this chapter will help parents avoid a sense of being out of control. Keeping the rules simple, being firm where necessary, taking the young person's needs into account, and keeping channels of communication open will all help to give parents a sense of being in control.

I want to tell a brief story to illustrate some of the points I have made in this chapter. The story concerns the troublesome issue of what to do with smart phones at night. A mother told me how she was worried that her daughter was staying up late at night, talking to her friends on her phone. The daughter was clearly tired in the mornings, and finding it hard to get up for school. The mother decided she would set the rule that, by 10.30 at night, her daughter should turn the phone off and leave it outside the bedroom.

This led to dramatic scenes of fury and resentment. There was much slamming of doors and yelling of abuse. However, the mother stood firm, and insisted that she was thinking of her daughter's welfare. On the second night the same thing happened, with more dramatic scenes. The same thing happened on the third night, by which time the mother was feeling anxious about whether she would be able to hold her ground.

On the fourth night the mother was amazed to see her daughter meekly put the phone outside her door and quietly get ready for bed! From that day onwards the question of what to do with the phone at night was never an issue. Many weeks later the daughter confessed that it was a great relief not to have her phone with her at night!

Conclusion

I will end the chapter with some tips from parents themselves.

- Stick to your guns.
  "Stick to your guns and prepare for the drama and accusations."
  This is all about being firm where necessary, even if it does mean tension and high emotion for a short while. The teenager may claim that rules and boundaries are terrible things. Yet they are absolutely essential. Young people need boundaries to be set by adults so that they can gradually incorporate them and in time set those boundaries and limits for themselves.
- Concentrate on one issue at a time.
  "I've found a good policy is to concentrate on one issue at a time. At the moment it's homework. As long as she does that I give her a lot of freedom in the other areas." This is linked to the idea of having as few rules as possible. Ask yourself what really matters, and concentrate on that.
- There are many ways to achieve your goal.
  "If you want something to go your way, the best way I feel is to suggest but not make the decision. Not say "We are going to do so and so", but to put it "What do you think about doing so and so?" Or "Do you think it would be a good idea?". This is about allowing the young person a say and a voice in decision-making. The more the teenager feels that her/his opinion is being listened to, the more likely it is that she/he will listen to the adult point of view.
- It doesn't always pay to win the argument.
  "Sometime there's nothing worse than when you've had a long argument with them and you finally produce an argument which

you know holds water, and that makes them even worse. You've shown them to be wrong, and they don't like that at all. It doesn't always pay to win the argument." This is about the power relationship. In this case the adult is trying to "win the argument". Yet what has been achieved? Communication with a teenager is not about who is right and who is wrong, but about sharing ideas and listening to each other.

- Encourage adult behaviour.

"If you give them the opportunity to make a suggestion that often works better than trying to force your ideas on them. Asking them what they think is encouraging adult behaviour, and that is what you're trying to encourage in teenagers." This is a really good point, and gets to the heart of what a parent is trying to achieve. Of course we want to keep them safe, and ensure that they do not go off the rails. But we also want to help them mature and grow up as responsible people. Helping them to make decisions and solve problems is one important way of doing that.

- They need guidance, but they don't need a straightjacket.

"It's difficult to know sometimes what they are asking for. It's up to the parent to understand what they're needing. They certainly need security. They need guidance, but they don't need a straightjacket." This parent describes the idea of the "authoritative parent" in one simple phrase. It is also a good place to end the chapter. Exercising parental authority during the teenage years is always going to be a balance between providing structure but allowing growth and development. A wise parent provides the guidance but avoids the straightjacket!

7

G – THE
GENERATION GAP

S - Significance
T – Two-way communication
A – Authority
G – Generation gap
E – Emotion

There are many reasons why parents and teenagers do not always see eye to eye. In the last chapters I have shown how differing ideas of authority and problems over communication can lead to conflict. In this chapter, I want to talk about the generation gap. This can be an important element in the overall picture of relationships between adults and young people.

The idea of a generation gap has a long history. Even Shakespeare, writing at the end of the sixteenth century, talked of young people as being at odds with the older generation. In modern times the idea of a generation gap refers to the possibility that adults and young people have different attitudes and values, whether these are about the internet, about mobile phones, or about the well-rehearsed subjects of sex and drugs.

> Everything's free nowadays – free sex and all the rest of it. I personally don't believe in free sex, but I am out of date. Sex is so available now, but I don't think it is good for teenagers. I think it causes more problems. My younger daughter talks very openly about it, and she says if she wants to sleep with someone then she will, whether I approve or not.
>
> (Mother of two daughters)

In this chapter, I want to explore the reasons for the generation gap, and how it affects relationships in the family. Time and time again in the interviews young people said that their parents made judgements about them based on the parents' own experiences of growing up. Young people believe this is unfair, as things today are different. Much has changed, and yet many adults make judgements about teenage behaviour according to standards from earlier times.

It's like the age difference. Where adults go: "back in my day", and stuff like that. Like so many things have changed, and they always go back to older times, but now we have all the computers, X boxes, play stations, phones and things, and like they always just go back to when they were young.

(15-year-old boy)

Yeah, because people like our parents grew up in a completely different world, well not completely different world, but a very different world to our generation, which has grown up with the internet, and you just see it as completely normal being able to access any piece of information whenever you feel like it, and yeah, my mum obviously grew up in a totally different world.

(16-year-old girl)

In this chapter, I want first to explore why the generation gap exists. Following that, I will look at some of the consequences of the generation gap. Finally, I will consider how parents and young people can reduce the gap, or at least acknowledge that it is acceptable to have different attitudes.

What causes the generation gap?

I suggest there are at least four reasons for the existence of this difference of attitude between the generations. In the first place it is obvious that parents of teenagers grew up in a different age compared with that experienced by their sons and daughters. I have already referred to such things as smart phones, the internet, and changed attitudes to sex. However, these are not the only social changes to affect young people's lives. The role of the media is different now, and the world of education has altered enormously over 40 years. Young people and young adults do not enter employment in the same way as was the case for previous generations. Teenagers' expectations of work and career are very different today, as are their experiences of friendship and the peer group as a result of social media.

57

Another important factor is simply that parents and teenagers are at different life stages. As one teenager put it: "They're at work, and we're not". As a result of this, the way people look at life is not going to be the same. Adults are carrying responsibilities for the family, and possibly for an extended family as well. Young people are focussed on their own lives, which certainly contain pressures, but of a very different sort. Thus attitudes and values may differ because of vastly differing life experiences.

> If one person has never worked, they may not understand the attitudes to employers and other people that the parent may have. Also money obviously. Even if the teenager is getting an allowance they are going to be dependent on their parents for that, which is quite difficult. How can you be emotionally independent when you're financially dependent? Teenagers now don't have a lot to look forward to workwise. Parents may not understand that. A lot of teenagers may feel: "What's the point of trying so hard, there are no jobs anyway". And parents want to push them to interviews and things where they haven't really got much chance. There is definitely a barrier there.
>
> (17-year-old boy)

A third possible reason for the generation gap has to do with the parents' difficulty in remembering what it was like when they were growing up. Many teenagers and parents mentioned this in the interviews. Parents recognised that they had largely forgotten their own adolescent years. A number of people remarked that, although everyone has gone through these years, few people use these memories to help them form good relationships with their teenagers.

> I think adults tend to forget about how they felt when they were younger. A lot of people seem to turn into their parents! When they were younger they were complaining about their parents, and then when they have their own kids they'll be doing the exact same thing that they complained about before! It's just interesting that they forget their ideas completely from when they were that age.
>
> (16-year-old boy)

Finally, there is something about the beliefs that parents have about appropriate teenage behaviour. I mentioned earlier that if parents are too forcible or unyielding in their judgements this makes conflict more likely. Many teenagers talked about the importance of not rushing to judgement before all the facts have been established. As one young woman put it when speaking about her parents:

> Non-judgemental is good, because you get judged from every angle all the time, and it is so good to have a place where you can talk and be open and not be judged.

As can be seen there are a variety of reasons which play a part in the development of a generation gap. These include:

- social change,
- parents and teenagers being at different life stages,
- parents not remembering what it was like when they were young,
- adults being overly judgemental about teenage behaviour.

All these contribute to the possibility that parents and young people will have differing attitudes and values. This is not necessarily a bad thing, and much can be done to reduce conflict between parents and teenagers. However, before looking at ways to reduce the gap between the generations, I want to consider briefly some of the consequences when teenagers believe that they are being judged unfairly.

Consequences of being judged

Many young people feel vulnerable and uncertain about themselves during the teenage years. Self-confidence can be shaky when an individual is experiencing major changes and going through a period of rapid development. Because of this it can be stressful to feel that you are being judged and criticised, and not surprisingly young people become defensive. Differences with parents over standards of behaviour can become a flashpoint for disagreement and conflict.

There are a number of consequences that flow from disagreements between the generations. In the first place, such disagreements contribute to a feeling on the part of the teenager that he or she is not respected by the parent. One of the things that teenagers want most is to be listened to, and to feel that their views are respected by the adults around them. High levels of conflict over standards and values can easily lead to a young person believing that their views are not being taken into account.

Following from this comes a feeling of resentment. Clearly, if the young person feels resentful about the way the parent is judging their behaviour, this can only lead to further conflict and bad feelings in the family.

Resentment in its turn can lead to problems in communication. As was noted in Chapter 5, one of the key elements which makes for good communication is the sense that each party is being listened to by the other. Talking and listening go hand in hand. This works well when young people feel that their viewpoint is being taken into account, and works badly when the opposite is the case. Clashes arising from differences in attitudes between the generations are likely to hinder communication.

Finally, and perhaps most important of all, this affects the degree of influence the parent has. The more disagreements there are, and the more problems there are over communication, the less influence the parents will have. To summarise, the consequences can run like this.

- teenager feels that their views are not respected. This leads to:
- teenager feeling resentment. This leads to:
- teenager being less inclined to be communicative about what is happening to them. This leads to:
- parent having less opportunity to be influential in the teenager's life.

I will now consider what can be done about this.

What can be done?

There is much that can be done, by both parents and young people, to reduce the negative impact of the generation gap. As I have said, the generation gap is not necessarily a bad thing. Open discussion and dialogue can be a healthy way for young people to learn and develop their own ideas. It can also help them recognise the importance of taking into account the feelings and beliefs of others. However, when discussion turns into conflict, and when this leads to communication breakdown, then the generation gap can cause serious problems.

Here are some tips from parents themselves.

- Realise that time's moved on.
  Most parents don't think they are old. When your children get to the point of wanting to do things that are alien to you, then you haven't realised that time's moved on. It's important to realise that in their eyes you are old. Society has

moved on, and parents have to try and be more aware of the fact that they are probably behind the times.

- Encourage them to talk.

  You've got to encourage them to talk to you about what their friends are doing, and see if you can glean from that whether they think their friends are doing the right or wrong thing. I think it's about trying to keep in touch with the sort of pressures that are on them, and whether you as a parent are in touch with today's teenage society. Whether we agree with it or not is another matter.

- Dredge up memories from your own teenage years.

  If you can, just remember times from your own teenage years. Try to dredge up a few memories. People say if you can put yourself in their position it will make things easier.

- Listen to yourself.

  I think one thing is to really stop and listen to yourself when you are having a go at them, and imagine being on the receiving end. It's quite an eye-opener!

- Show respect for each other's views.

  This is probably the most important tip of all. It is hard for parents to stand back, and refrain from taking control. It is especially hard if parents are anxious that the young person will get into difficulty or come to harm. Yet, as we have seen, the two generations will have different views, and it will help if each can respect the other. As teenagers grow older they will develop their own ideas, and they will be influenced by their own generation. This is what one 15-year-old said when asked what advice he would give to parents.

Just really try to understand young people better. Not necessarily to join in with their lifestyle, but maybe ask questions about what the teenager enjoys doing without pressing for information. Just respect the person as an individual.

8

E – EMOTION

S – Significance
T – Two-way communication
A – Authority
G – Generation gap
E – Emotion

This is the final chapter in my description of the STAGE framework. In this chapter, I want to consider the impact of emotions on the relationships between parent and teenager. This is a topic of great importance. It was constantly referred to in the interviews. However, it is often very hard to stand back and get these feelings into perspective. I believe that if parents can learn to manage some of the difficult feelings that they experience, this will be helpful in giving them a greater sense of confidence.

In this chapter, I will consider the emotions of parents, but we should not ignore the fact that the emotions of teenagers also play a part in the overall picture. Indeed it could be claimed that it is precisely because the emotions of teenagers are all over the place during this stage that the emotions of parents are similarly affected. There is no secret about the fact that many teenagers go through periods when their feelings are difficult to regulate. Words like "moody" and "emotional" are commonly used to describe teenage behaviour.

> They are not always in control of their emotions. I think they quite alarm themselves by some of the emotions they are feeling. I think their emotions do swing. You can't really be very logical about emotions, they are just very strong feelings. In fact if you asked a teenager how they could go from one feeling to its very opposite so quickly, I don't know if they could actually explain.
>
> (Mother of two daughters)

In the chapter, it will be important first to set out a little about the emotional life of the teenager. Following this I will consider some of the feelings experienced by parents. Love for the teenager is central of course, but I will also look at emotions such as frustration and irritation, as well as sadness, guilt, and loss. The chapter will then conclude with a discussion of how best to manage strong feelings between parents and teenagers.

The emotions of teenagers

In Chapter 2, when describing brain development, I referred to the area called the amygdala. This is the site in the brain that manages emotions, sensations, and arousal. This area undergoes major change during the teenage years, and takes some time to settle down. At times it can be a very powerful force. This means it can be difficult for young people to regulate their emotions. The amygdala is very much affected by the hormone balance, and there will be times when this is extremely volatile. As a result the teenager can experience great swings from one mood to another.

I also talked about the transition, and the flip-flop of emotions as being one feature of the change from child to adult. I talked about the fact that, as is stated in the quote above, emotions can fluctuate from one extreme to the other. I suggested that this was as much to do with the uncertainty of the transition as it was to do with the changes occurring as part of puberty and brain development.

Thus there are many factors that will affect young people and their ability to control their emotions. Three of these are:

- brain development,
- the hormonal balance,
- the social and emotional changes that are part of the journey from childhood to adulthood.

It is important to recognise that young people themselves are acutely aware of the difficulty in managing their emotions. Many teenagers described feelings that were uncomfortable for them. Here are two examples.

> I think a lot of kids are a bit confused at adolescence because there are a lot of changes in the body, and a lot in the mind too. When I was about 10 my Mum gave me a book about what would happen during adolescence, mentally as well as

physically. I was reading about "Oh, you'll quite often feel depressed. You won't really know why. Most people don't like how their bodies turn out". I was thinking what a load of rubbish!. But I did get really ratty and grumpy for a year or so.

(15-year-old girl)

When I'm with certain people I tend to feel pressured. If I'm with people I feel inferior to I tend to feel very quiet and trapped. I'm very on my guard about what I do and say. I don't want to appear silly. When I'm with a boy I get really nervous. I'm not inclined to talk. I'm more inclined to snap back answers and pretend I'm not there, and hope he'll go away, although I really do want to talk to him.

(16-year-old girl)

There is no doubt that this can be a time for many young people when their feelings are particularly strong, while also being difficult to control. Mood swings, pressure and tension, anxiety, worry: all these part of the growing up process. Of course adults have these feelings too, but with maturity comes a greater ability to manage emotion.

It is important also to note that there are very wide individual differences. Many factors play a part in how young people deal with their feelings, and how this affects relationships. One element that was mentioned by many parents was the question of gender.

Boys are just so much easier. They don't hang their problems out like a girl would. A girl could sulk for a week, and won't talk to you, and refuses to do anything, while a boy, within 10 minutes of you shouting at them they'll come back in and say: "Any chance you can make a sandwich?". And it's like they're completely different.

(Mother of a son and daughter)

Not everyone took this view, and some parents found boys more difficult than girls. Boys, it was argued, tend to shut themselves away when they are upset, whereas girls will at least let everyone know how they are feeling. Also of course there are differences between individuals. Two girls in a family can be radically different in the way they handle emotion. One can become babyish and needy, whilst another can push the parent away, preferring to manage things on their own.

All this is an important background to understanding the emotional life of the parent. Living with a teenager whose emotions are raw and out in the open can be stressful in itself. Not only that, but it is only human to respond to one emotion with another. In a relationship it is easy for one person to be rational when the other person is being rational too. However, when one person is expressing strong feelings, this is bound to influence the other person. Add to that the worry about how best to parent a growing and developing young person, and it is not difficult to see why emotion is such an important topic if we want to understand parent-teenager relationships.

The emotions of parents

Many parents worry about the strength of their feelings, whether these are anger, anxiety, shame, or guilt. Many believe that, in some way, it is their fault that they have such powerful emotions. Of course parents play their part, but it is important to realise that the emotions of a son or daughter will have their effect too. Both sides influence each other. It is for this reason that relationships are a two-way street.

In this section, I am first going to consider one of the most common emotions, which is anger in its many forms. It may be expressed as irritation, frustration, upset, stress, or plain fury. Clearly not everyone has these feelings, but in the interviews there were certainly a number of parents who wanted to talk about the anger and resentment they felt towards their teenager. Most frequently the anger was generated as a result of conflict, or because of behaviour which was seen as unacceptable. Parents also talked of being upset by rudeness and what was called a "disrespectful attitude". One or two parents used the word "hate", always adding that they needed to tell their teenager that they loved them too.

> I get such strong feelings, I mean quite often I've said: "I love you, but I hate the way you behave". Of course she reads that the wrong way. "You hate me, you love my brother more". So you do have to be careful how you say it, don't you? Anyway it doesn't get you anywhere, does it?
>
> (Mother of three teenagers)

At the end of the chapter I will talk about how to manage emotions that occur in a relationship with a teenager. Here it is just worth saying that to have such strong feelings of anger and frustration is very upsetting. It is essential to stand back, and ask yourself why this is happening. Talking to other people can also help.

Emotions such as this are likely to have a damaging effect on the relationship. You may believe it is all the teenager's fault, but that does not make things any easier. Try to get some distance, and some perspective on the situation. Is your teenager as angry as you are? If so, why? However painful, think about your own role. Is there anything you can do to reduce the tension, and help the teenager with their own confusing and upsetting feelings?

It is difficult to talk about strong emotions. Not everyone can own up to feeling angry or furious with their son or daughter. It takes courage to acknowledge these feelings to yourself, let alone to other people. However, there are some emotions that are even harder to face up to. I will discuss three of these now, namely sadness, shame, and guilt.

This mother was asked what her main feeling was about her parenting a teenager.

> Oh my god, I would probably say disappointment, that we didn't have a better relationship. She is distant from me, so it is a little bit sad for me. I do feel that. It's sad, but I'm hoping that she will come back to me one day.... She needs a lot of space, a good 5-foot radius, and yes, it is a bit sad really. I've just got to hold on to the fact that she's clever, she's pretty, and she's good away from the home.
>
> (Mother of one daughter)

Among the various emotions that are experienced during the teenage years, a sense of loss is one that almost all parents experience at one time or another. This can be harder for some parents than for others. In the case quoted above, this mother was left with sadness and disappointment, while for other parents the sense of loss can be accompanied by pride or pleasure as a result of the young person's achievements.

Growing up inevitably means growing away from the family. However, the extent of the break varies enormously depending on so many factors, particularly gender and personality. Some teenagers remain close to their parents, even though they gradually acquire greater independence. Others may seek to live away from their parents, making new relationships and keeping only a tenuous link with their birth family. One of the most difficult aspects of being a parent is being able to let go, and come to terms with the loss that is a part of being a mother or father of a teenager.

One or two parents talked of emotions such as shame or guilt. In these cases particular circumstances had led to parents having these painful feelings. Some parents talked of serious behaviour problems, while others discussed the emotions caused by having a son or daughter with learning difficulties or other special needs. Here is one example of a mother whose daughter had gone through a troubled time during her teenage years.

> One of the most difficult things is when you meet someone who's got a child of the same age and they say: "How's she doing?". And you've got to turn round and say: "I don't want to talk about it". Or you tell them the truth where the pride part of you just wants to say: "Oh terrific, she's got so many GCSEs, and A levels and stuff, and she's doing this and she's doing that". But you can't, because she's not doing any of these things, and you feel ashamed, and yet another part of you will feel, well, I don't know, maybe she will grow out of it. It's in all of us, this pride in our children. We want to say they're doing well. We want them to do what we want them to do. We want to be proud of them. Then you find out that what you've got on your hands is someone who doesn't really want to do any of the things you want them to do.
>
> (Mother of three)

Emotions play a highly significant role in family life. At no time is this more relevant than during the teenage years. In spite of this, it is often hard for parents and teenagers to acknowledge their feelings, even though these may be getting in the way of talking or making sensible decisions. One of the main conclusions I would like you to draw from this chapter is that acknowledging your emotions, and learning to manage them, can make a significant difference to how you play your role as a parent of a teenager.

Before I go on to suggest some tips about how to manage emotions, it is important to note that, in this discussion of emotions and feelings, I have not yet mentioned love. A whole book could be written about a parent's love for their child, and many authors have done just this. *Why love matters* by Sue Gerhardt is a good example, although her focus is on the early years, and not on adolescence. This leads me on to say that it is a lot easier to talk about love when we think of young children, and a lot harder to talk about love when we are thinking about teenagers.

Teenagers need love just as much as younger children do, but they need it to be expressed in a different way. In the interviews many parents talked about how they understood love as it applies to teenagers. Here are two examples.

> They need support, continuity. I think they need you always to be around, to be a rock so that they can go out and come back and you'll always be there.
>
> (Mother of two)

> I think that, although they don't realise it, they need a lot of love in the teenage years. It's the sort of love that stands back and helps, not takes over.
>
> (Mother of four)

There are many ways of showing that you love your teenage son or daughter. How this works in your family will depend partly on your own style of showing love, and partly on the teenager's reactions and responses to parental affection. Every teenager will have slightly differing needs, and it will be important for a parent to be sensitive to this.

Love and affection can be demonstrated through care and concern, through taking a genuine interest in the things the teenager is interested in, by being available at times of stress, and so on. Perhaps the most important lesson of all is to recognise that your daughter or son needs just as much love during the teenage years as she or he did during childhood.

Conclusion

I will end the chapter with some tips from parents as they were expressed in the interviews.

- "That's the hard bit, I find, just walk away and calm down".
  This mother attended a parents' group, as she was having terrible rows with her son. She recalled how she gradually learnt to stand back, take a deep breath, and calm down. If she could do this before getting into more discussion with her son, it avoided further arguments. However, she did also say that this is a hard thing to do. It needs practice, but it can be done. Learning to breathe deeply, and to turn away for a short time, can make all the difference.

- "Sense of humour, and remembering how I felt at that age".

  This mother talks about the important role of humour, but she also talks about trying to recall the pressures she was under when she was a teenager. She tells the interviewer that, for her, this helps to put things into perspective, and to realise that: "there is a tomorrow, and it is not the end of the world if things do not go right today". This is also about being able to see what the world looks like from the teenager's point of view. What emotions are they experiencing? Are they angry, upset, or under stress? If you want to understand your own feelings it can help enormously to try and stand in the other person's shoes.

- "I think the more you talk to people, you realise that it's just what teenagers do".

  This is all about sharing experiences, and learning that other parents are going through the same things as you are yourself. It is very easy to get into a mindset where you feel that your teenager is doing things to spite you. The experience of dealing with an angry teenager can leave you feeling isolated and alone. If you can find ways of talking to others, and learning that you are not alone, it will make it easier to put your own feelings into perspective.

- "As parents you have to be consistent, and understand where one needs to rock in, and one needs to stop".

  This parent is talking about the relationship between two adults in the parenting role. I have already referred to this in the section on co-parenting. Whether the parents are living together or apart, it will be a lot easier to manage difficult emotions if, on the one hand, there is some consistency between the couple, and, on the other, if each parent can play a slightly different role. This parent puts if well by talking about one rocking in and one standing back. This hints at good cooperation between the couple, one supporting the other when things get difficult. This is not always possible, as parents may not agree about how to handle a challenging teenager. Nonetheless, cooperation and respect between the two parents can make it a lot easier to manage strong emotions in the family.

I have now come to the end of Part I of this book. I will now turn to Part II, in which you will find chapters on topics of general concern such as health, sex, the digital world, and so on. In each of these chapters I will refer to the STAGE framework, showing how it can be applied to the various topics covered.

Part II

9

TEENAGERS AND HEALTH

The topic of health has already been the subject of discussion in previous sections of the book. Chapter 2 on the brain represents one perspective on teenage health. This included growth and maturation, the role of hormones, emotion regulation, and other subjects that could all be considered to be aspects of health and development. Puberty was also something I discussed earlier, another factor that is intrinsically tied up with health during this stage.

I now want to turn to some other aspects of health which play an important role in the teenage years. I also want to show how the STAGE framework can help us to understand health issues. In this chapter I will include brief sections on:

- exercise,
- eating,
- sleep,
- mental health,
- smoking, drugs, and alcohol.

Of course each of these topics is complex, and probably deserves a chapter on its own. For those who want to discover more, I will have some suggestions for further resources at the end of the book.

The STAGE framework and health

There are many ways in which the framework can be useful for parents and carers in the way they deal with health issues. Here are just a few examples. First, the S for "significance" is critical here. All the evidence shows that adult behaviour has a big impact on the health of young people around them. How adults use alcohol or drugs, their eating habits, or their attitudes to exercise will all influence the way teenagers behave. Adults are role models, but they also can provide support and guidance at key moments where health is concerned. Parents and carers are significant in relation to health just as much as they are in relation to other aspects of life.

Communication is important too. If communication is one-way, with adults being directive about health issues, then the opportunities for support and guidance will be lessened. If communication can be two-way, there is more chance that the young person will hear what the adult is saying and be able to accept support. The E for "emotion" also has a part to play. Health issues can generate strong and difficult emotions. Eating, sleep, or sex can all become battle fields in the ongoing relationships between parents and teenagers. How these emotions are managed will have an influence on the ways teenagers learn to take control of themselves and their health behaviours. These are just a few examples of how the STAGE framework can help in understanding teenagers and health.

Exercise

The first thing to say is that, as most people are aware, exercise is a good thing. Healthy exercise has a wide range of benefits, including strengthening the cardiovascular system, promoting bone and muscle growth, moderating body weight, countering depression, and (for most sports) encouraging social contact. There has been much concern in recent years over the possibility that young people are taking less exercise today than was the case in the past. Teenagers are now less likely to walk or cycle to school, and there are more restrictions in the amount of outdoor activities which are available to this age group.

Two other trends have heightened anxieties about low levels of exercise: the first is the increased use of the car for travel, and the second is the attraction of screen time, whether that involves watching television, playing electronic games, or using the internet. Interestingly, research shows that exercise levels for teenagers have not dropped markedly over the last 20 years, but have remained broadly similar, with a slight increase in time spent in exercise during the early years of the twenty-first century. The negative impact of the sale of school playing fields has been countered by government policy requiring schools to provide at least a certain level of physical activity for pupils during the school day.

While levels of exercise in general have not gone down in the recent past, there is certainly a big change following puberty. As parents will be aware, the amount of exercise taken by teenagers decreases as they get older. This trend is most noticeable for girls, but is also true for many boys as well. Over the 5-year period from age 11 to age 16 the number of young people taking physical exercise falls by about 10% for boys, but by about 25% for girls.

Why should this be so? Teenagers give a number of reasons as to why they lose interest in sport and other exercise. These include:

- not getting better – no evidence of improvement or achievement,
- conflict of interest – other activities being more interesting,
- too much pressure from adults – particularly from a coach or PE teacher,
- lack of time – school work and social activities take precedence,
- boredom – a lack of interest in the activity itself.

In addition, there are two reasons that may be of special importance to some girls. These are:

- the social context of sport – negative peer pressure towards girls who play sport,
- the physical nature of sport – girls not wanting to get sweaty, to go into changing rooms, and to get involved in the sort of bonding that seems to be part of sporting activity.

All these reasons are perfectly legitimate, and show how sport and exercise fit in to other teenage concerns. These include the wish to be accepted by the peer group, the need to do things that provide an opportunity to improve or achieve, and the general busy-ness of teenage life. There is of course an important gender aspect to this topic. Sport is still very much a male activity, in spite of a higher profile being given today to female sportswomen. For teenage boys there are many positives that come from being engaged in sport, while this is less so for girls. In particular the physical development of the body following puberty has an impact here. For many girls breast development and menstruation can feel as if they get in the way of sport, while for boys their bodies are more suited to many sporting activities. In addition, boys who are good at sport are more popular in the peer group, while for girls the opposite often applies.

It is notable, however, that in the last few years there has been a change in public attitudes to women in sport. The mainstream media are giving more attention to women's competitions, and there is more evidence of girls playing sports such as football and rugby, sports that were considered a male preserve until a few years ago. It is to be hoped that this shift in attitudes will encourage young women to see sport as something that can be as important for them as it is for young men.

There are many reasons why engagement in sport and exercise can provide rewards for teenagers. These include:

- skill – to gain a feeling of accomplishment or ability,
- social – to gain a sense of belonging to a social group,
- fitness – to improve body image, strength, and stamina,
- competition – to perform well in a particular domain,
- enjoyment – to have fun, or to gain a sense of vitality, happiness, and well-being.

To conclude this section, it is worth considering what parents can do to encourage a teenager to take more exercise. In the first place all the points noted above can be suggested as possible reasons to be involved in sport and exercise. As with so many things, opening this topic up for discussion is an important thing to do. The more sport and exercise is talked about in the family, the more the teenager will learn about the relation between exercise and good health. Furthermore, it is obviously important to recognise that taking regular exercise does not necessarily mean getting involved in team sports. Activities such as cycling, skating, running, and swimming can all be organised to suit the individual, and without the demands and social pressures of sports at school.

In addition to all this, there is one further consideration. As I have noted in discussing the STAGE framework, parents are role models. The amount of exercise taken by a teenager may be influenced by the behaviour of the parent. If the parent is willing to show an example, and to take exercise themselves, then this may have more of an impact than any good advice. Best of all, if the parent can organise things so that they can take exercise with the teenager, this can become an important shared activity. In this situation, actions speak louder than words!

Eating and nutrition

Food and food intake have an obvious relevance to the health of a teenager. There are many reasons for this. In the first place puberty brings with it major changes in the shape and size of the body. These changes are not always easy to cope with. As what we eat affects our body size and shape, a teenager can use the amount of food they eat as a way of controlling how their body develops. If they wish to be smaller or slimmer then they may restrict their eating, whereas if they wish to be bigger and stronger they may increase their food intake.

Second, there has been much discussion of the role of the media here, and of the promotion of "the perfect body". Many teenagers are extremely sensitive to the way they look, and wish to be popular with the peer group. As a result it is believed that media images put pressure on girls to be slimmer and boys to be full of muscle. This in turn affects the way young people eat, possibly leading to dieting or over-eating.

Third, teenagers may prefer certain foods, such as pizza, which is consumed less often by adults. This can be a means of establishing an adolescent identity. In this way food preferences for teenagers can be a "lifestyle choice", enabling them to be seen as separate and different. However, this has an impact on nutrition. The result can be positive, as for example choosing to be vegetarian, but it is not so positive for health if the preference is for fast foods. Crisps, burgers, pizzas, and fizzy drinks are consumed more by teenagers than by adults, and this has led to anxiety over the long-term impact of such foods on health and body weight.

It is well-known that high levels of sugar and certain fats contained in fast foods are damaging to health. Obesity is a worldwide concern for public health specialists, but it is of particular concern for those interested in adolescent nutrition. The drive to increase awareness of healthy eating has had some impact in recent years, but levels of obesity among children and young people show no signs of diminishing.

It is important to state that it is not just teenagers who have shown an increase in obesity in recent years. Obesity has increased among all age groups, and there are many possible reasons for this. The most likely reason is that economic growth, particularly in the Western world, has made possible a greater availability of all types of foods. This inevitably means that people eat more. Other possible reasons for obesity may include genetic factors, lower levels of exercise, and the increased intake of fatty or sugary foods.

Turning now to the other side of the coin, restricting food intake by dieting or slimming is a common form of behaviour among teenagers. Some studies show that as many as 40 per cent or even 50 per cent of teenage girls in the 14 to 16 years age range are dieting or trying to limit what they eat. Why should this be so?

First, it is worth noting that many adult women diet. One possible reason for teenage dieting, therefore, is that young people are simply following the role models they see around them. This would of course extend to the media as well. Another factor here relates to the physical changes taking place in early adolescence. These changes can be disturbing. They rarely lead to the ideal shape and size, so that young people may go through a stage of feeling worried and dissatisfied with their own bodies. Eating less, and hoping to be slim, may be part of that dissatisfaction with the body that is so common among teenage girls.

There is of course a big difference between dieting and having an eating disorder. The two most common eating disorders are anorexia and bulimia. The characteristics of anorexia include significant weight loss, a morbid fear of becoming fat, a distorted body image, and periods stopping. Bulimia by contrast involves binge eating and a lack of control over eating behaviour. Pointers to further information about eating disorders can be found at the end of the book.

The most important questions for parents are: "How can I tell the difference between dieting and anorexia? When should I be worried?".

There is no simple answer to these questions. It is always a good idea to consult your GP or other health professional if you are worried. It is useful to remember that, as far as an eating disorder is concerned, it is not only weight loss that is significant. Parents often concentrate on weight, and weight loss, but other physical and psychological signs will be important in the overall picture.

In terms of weight, every person is different. There are scales available which indicate the range of normal weight for an individual's size. These are known as body mass index (BMI) scales. These should be consulted to get an idea of how an individual teenager compares with others of similar age and height. However, serious weight loss is usually a clear indication of an eating disorder.

Some of the other signs of an eating disorder are as follows:

- an alteration in eating patterns or persistence of an unusual pattern of eating,
- an increased preoccupation with food,
- a loss of, or failure to start periods,
- secrecy around food,
- a morbid fear of gaining weight,
- a distorted body image,
- constant self-criticism,
- social withdrawal.

I would stress that these signs can only be taken as a general indication of the sorts of things to look out for. If a parent is worried about an eating disorder it is essential to consult a health professional. Turning to the question of how to distinguish an eating disorder from dieting, the following things should be borne in mind. Most people who diet only manage to lose small amounts of weight, so severe weight loss has to be taken seriously. Most people who diet are not secretive about it, they do not have a distorted body image, and they do not show major changes in the way they think about food. These considerations should be helpful for parents if they are worried about their teenager's eating behaviour.

Sleep

For many families getting teenagers to go to sleep at night can be the cause of considerable friction. It is often assumed that young people are being difficult when they say they cannot sleep. Parents may think that teenagers stay up late as they want to continue using the internet or the phone to keep in touch with friends, or that they use night time to do things they do not want their parents to know about. At the other end of the spectrum all of us will recognise the image of the teenager who sleeps till lunchtime on the weekend.

In the first chapter I mentioned sleep as one of the topics that has been the subject of important new research in recent years. In essence this research has shown that, following the onset of puberty, the system in the brain that governs sleep patterns changes during early adolescence.

The mechanism which makes us sleepy, in part controlled by the hormone melatonin, is delayed. This leads to a situation where many teenagers take longer to feel sleepy. There is approximately a two-hour delay in the release of melatonin during the early adolescent years. Scientists have talked about teenagers as "owls" rather than "larks". What was once thought of as contrary adolescent behaviour can now be seen to have a biological basis.

There are many implications of this research. In the first place it is clear that teenagers need a good night's sleep. Health professionals suggest that nine hours sleep should be the norm for most young people between the ages of 11 and 17. When teenagers were put in a laboratory and allowed to sleep as much as they liked, the average sleep time was 9.5 hours. However, if someone takes a long time to go to sleep, and then wakes at 7.00 a.m. because of the school day, they will be missing out on sleep. This is one of the reasons why teenagers get up later on weekends. They are catching up on much needed sleep.

Schools in parts of the USA, and one or two schools in Britain, have considered starting the school day later, so that pupils will have sufficient sleep. What little evidence we have shows an improvement in exam results in such schools. It is not surprising, however, that the system is not popular with parents or with teachers, as it is too disruptive of other routines and work patterns.

Recent research has also highlighted that sleep is important for learning as well as for rest. It appears that sleep is a time for what is called memory consolidation. In other words all the learning that has taken place during the day is organised, sorted, and laid down in long-term memory during the hours of sleep. Serious lack of sleep therefore affects not only moods and behaviour, it also has an impact on learning.

I cannot stress too strongly that teenagers need sufficient and regular sleep. We know that young people who regularly get less than six hours sleep at night will be at a serious disadvantage. There is much that parents can do to help teenagers develop healthy sleep patterns. Here are some suggestions:

- talk about sleep with your teenager, emphasising how important it is for good health,
- help your teenager to get into a routine at night,
- insist that phones are left outside the bedroom, that lights are dimmed, and that there is no use of the internet after a certain time,
- if a teenager cannot get to sleep, work together on possible strategies to encourage drowsiness, such as having a hot drink, listening to slow music, and so on,
- do not criticise a teenager for wanting to sleep in on weekends.

Mental health

Mental health in adolescence is a complex topic. It will only be possible in this short section to cover some general aspects of the subject. Mental health problems range widely, and include conditions such as schizophrenia, anxiety states, obsessive compulsive disorder (OCD), autism and Asperger's syndrome, and suicide and self-harm. To understand these fully it will be necessary for readers to consult more specialised resources, as well as referring to organisations such as the charity Young Minds. If a parent is worried about a son or daughter, it is essential to seek professional advice. Here I will consider some of the common worries of parents, and outline what parents can do to help and support teenagers if they experience stressful times.

The first thing to explore is the definition of a mental health problem. What exactly is meant by this term? I have already referred to the difference between dieting and an eating disorder, and this is helpful in considering the broader question. The criteria used to define an eating disorder are as follows:

- a significant change in behaviour,
- a marked physical change, such as serious weight loss,
- evidence of unusual emotional states, such as preoccupations, fears, or anxieties that did not exist beforehand.

It is important to stress that it is the overall picture that has to be taken into account, rather than any one sign or symptom. Many teenagers may have difficulty in one area, but be able to function well in other areas. To be able to say that someone has a mental health problem it is essential to consider the picture as a whole.

A commonly accepted definition of a mental health problem is a set of clinically recognisable symptoms or behaviours, linked with distress or interference with personal functioning of at least two weeks' duration. The definition of a mental health problem is closely linked with the question many parents ask: "How do I know if this is normal adolescence or something more serious?".

Four considerations are helpful here.

- the length of time the problem has persisted,
- the severity of the symptoms,
- the extent to which the problem is interfering with the young person's life,
- the extent to which the problem is affecting the family more broadly.

As a general rule, if the problem has lasted some time (more than two weeks), if the symptoms are serious, and if the functioning of the young person and/or the family is being affected, then professional help will be needed.

A discussion of depression might be useful as an illustration of some of these points. Many young people have times when they feel sad or miserable. As I have noted, mood swings are common among teenagers. This does not mean that a teenager is suffering from depression. Only a very few become ill with this condition. Research tells us that roughly 10 per cent of the adolescent population can be said to have clinical depression at some time, while between 20 per cent and 30 per cent experience low mood at one time or another.

There are many different symptoms of depression, ranging from sadness, misery, and feelings of hopelessness on the one hand, to disturbed sleep patterns, poor eating, self-harm, and suicidal thoughts and behaviours on the other. Clearly, the latter group of symptoms are more serious than the former.

If this information is applied to the earlier discussion, it can be seen that to say that someone is seriously depressed it is necessary to identify at least some of the following:

- that the individual has been feeling sad or hopeless over a period of time,
- that the individual's symptoms are serious, and difficult to control or modify,
- that the individual's daily functioning (such as eating, sleeping, or going to school) has been affected,
- that the individual's behaviour has changed, that is from being sociable to becoming isolated.

I want to consider now what parents can do to provide support for a teenager if he or she is experiencing mental health problems. The first and most obvious thing to say is that it is enormously important for parents to be well-informed. There are useful resources to be found at the end of the book. One of the problems regarding mental ill-health is that there is generally a low level of public understanding. Yet a variety of resources can be found on the internet which provide good quality information. The more parents know, the easier it will be for them to offer the right support.

This lack of understanding is closely related to the stigma associated with mental health. If people feel ashamed of mental ill-health it means that they are unwilling to talk about it, and hesitant about seeking help. There is also the fear that mental ill-health is closely linked to madness. This adds to the anxiety, and makes people cautious about sharing their concerns with others. It will be helpful if parents can do everything in their power to counteract any stigma about mental health. They should make sure that their son or daughter receives fair treatment from schools and other agencies.

Finally, all the things that have already been said about effective parenting for teenagers will apply in double measure to those with mental health problems. The provision of support by parents will involve:

- recognising rather than denying the problem,
- trying to get the best professional help available,
- looking for positives, and bolstering self-esteem,

- starting from the position of the young person, rather than imposing adult solutions to solve the problem.

Smoking, drugs, and alcohol

In this last section, I will consider the effects of the use of these different substances, all of which can play an important part in the lives of teenagers. Dealing first with smoking, it is encouraging to note that the use of tobacco among young people has been decreasing steadily over the last 20 years. This is in line with adult trends, and has been influenced by government policy and by pricing strategies. Recent research showed that approximately one in five 15-year-olds have smoked at some time, with girls smoking more than boys.

As far as the reasons for smoking are concerned, it has been shown that smoking rates are higher in families where parents or siblings smoke, and as a result of anxiety and low self-esteem. It is not clear why smoking is more popular among girls than among boys. One possible theory is that smoking is considered by young women to be linked to diet and weight control. Interestingly, the gender difference disappears after the age of 16. There are no differences in rates of smoking in the 16–19 years age group, nor in adult populations.

Turning now to drugs, this is the area of risk that causes more worry for parents than almost any other. I will try and concentrate here on some of the facts that will help parents get this subject into perspective. First, it is very important to emphasise that not all drugs are the same. When someone talks about teenagers and drugs, the first question to ask is: "What drugs are we talking about?".

Smoking a joint of cannabis at a party is not the same as being a regular user of cocaine or heroin. To give an example of the frequency of use, studies show that somewhere in the region of 25 per cent of teenagers aged 16 have used cannabis at some time, whereas the proportion of 16-year-olds using a drug such as heroin is less than 2 per cent. Cannabis may be illegal, but its use is far more widespread than the use of other drugs. There is a big difference between addiction and experimentation in a leisure context.

There are many different ways to classify drugs, and it has to be noted that these classifications do change over time. Cannabis is a good example, as its classification has been altered by various governments depending on attitudes to this drug. At the time of writing, the UK Government uses the following classification for illegal drugs:

- class A – cocaine, heroin, and ecstasy,
- class B – cannabis and amphetamines,
- class C – tranquilisers and steroids.

As can be seen, this classification indicates the level of danger associated with each drug, and the penalties for possession and dealing are linked to this classification.

A word about cannabis is necessary here. Many parents who grew up in the 1970s and 1980s considered cannabis to be a safe drug, with no harmful effects. Indeed it was often said that cannabis was less harmful that alcohol. However, since the 1990s new types of cannabis have become available. These types of cannabis have a much higher level of the active ingredient in them, and are thus more dangerous. It is now known that regular cannabis use (three times a week or more) can lead to serious mental health problems.

What can parents do if they are worried? The first thing to do is to establish what drugs are being used, and in what context. If a teenager is only using a drug such as cannabis very occasionally, at a party or special event, then it will be important not to over-react. There should be an open discussion to ensure that the teenager has all the facts about cannabis, and knows how to keep safe. If, however, it appears that the drug use is of a more serious nature, then a different approach will be necessary.

Serious drug use is similar to other mental health problems, in that the individual will need help to deal with the problem. Parents should seek professional advice, as well as making every attempt to support the young person in breaking the habit. It will certainly be the case that other aspects of the young person's life, such as school work and friendships, will be affected by this use of drugs. I will have more to say about serious drug use in Chapter 14 when I deal with challenging behaviour.

Finally, how can parents recognise a drug habit? The answer to this is similar to that given about any mental health problem. The following signs may be helpful:

- a marked change in behaviour,
- physical signs such as poor eating, weight loss, difficulty in sleeping, or a change in physical appearance,
- being secretive about activities,
- a change in friendship group, or increase in social isolation,
- a loss of interest in activities that were previously important to the individual.

The last area to deal with in this section is alcohol. There has been much comment recently about the increase in drinking among young people. By the age of 16 almost all teenagers will have tasted alcohol, and many will have been to parties where excessive amounts of alcohol are consumed. It is certainly the case that alcohol is now much easier to obtain, as it is available in supermarkets and corner stores. Research shows that those who do drink are likely to consume more alcohol than was the case in the past.

Why do teenagers drink? Here are some possible reasons:

- to feel grown up,
- to feel happy,
- to become relaxed in social situations,
- to rebel,
- because of social pressure,
- to get up courage to approach someone they fancy.

It is probably the case that a combination of reasons will be at the root of adolescent drinking, some of which are of course very similar to those affecting adult drinking. This leads on to the important point that, in many cases, young people are simply doing the same as adults. It is essential for adults to avoid hypocrisy here. Adults who drink heavily themselves should think twice before giving lectures to young people about the dangers of alcohol!

Of course parents do worry about their teenager's safety, and there is no doubt that consumption of alcohol, especially at parties, is a cause for concern. There are some things that parents can do. These include making sure that the young person is properly informed about safe drinking, providing information about the units of alcohol in each drink, and being a role model for safe drinking themselves.

In spite of all this, and however much parents do, the truth is that almost all teenagers will get drunk at some time. In part this is a "rite of passage", something that young people need to do as part of the growing up process. For this reason it is doubly important that parents do not hide their heads in the sand. Most young people will drink with their friends, so thinking through how to be as safe as possible is really worthwhile. Here are some thoughts about how young people can be as safe as possible when drinking in social situations.

- Drink beers or wines which have lower levels of alcohol, rather than spirits or cocktails.

- Drink slowly, making one drink last a long time.
- Be aware of what is in your drink, and keep an eye open in case anything extra is added.
- Get rid of a drink you do not like.
- Pay for your own drinks.
- Never drink on an empty stomach.
- Never drink too much when you are alone.
- Refuse a lift from someone who has been drinking.
- Always make sure you have enough money for a taxi home.
- Be careful not to drink if you are taking any medication.

Conclusion

In this chapter I have covered some of the more obvious issues to do with young people's health. While most teenagers could be described as healthy, there are a small number who suffer from health problems such diabetes, asthma, or other long-term conditions. These young people will need ongoing medical help. For the majority health matters are more routine, but this does not mean they should be ignored. The more parents can be informed, the more they will be able to provide reassurance and advice when young people have concerns about their health. As I have mentioned, further information on individual health topics will be found at the end of the book.

10

SEX AND GENDER

In the interviews we carried out one 15-year-old girl said: "My parents don't want to talk about anything else! They are always asking me: 'Am I doing it yet?' They may be obsessed with sex, but I'm not!".

It is understandable that parents do worry about this. An unwanted pregnancy, a sexually transmitted infection, or even just being under pressure to have sex when you are not ready are all realistic things to worry about where teenage girls are concerned. On the other hand it will be obvious that, as a parent, you will not want to give your daughter, or your son, the impression that you are "obsessed with sex".

This is a topic that has always been tricky for parents of teenagers. However, so much has changed in the last couple of decades that sexual behaviour today poses quite new challenges. I have called this chapter "Sex and gender" for the very good reason that gender identity, and the growing visibility of transgender youth, has raised key questions about adolescent sexual development. In addition sex has become possible in a new world – the on-line world. I will be referring later to a research project entitled *Digital romance*. In addition to all this, sexual behaviour appears to be changing, with surveys indicating that teenagers are having sex at a later age today than was the case 15 or 20 years ago.

In this chapter, I will first discuss the STAGE framework and show how this relates to sex and gender. I will go on to consider:

- gender identity,
- early sexual relationships,
- digital romance,
- contraception,
- gay, lesbian, and bi-sexual relationships,
- sex and the law.

I will conclude with some tips to address the fears and anxieties of both parents and teenagers.

The STAGE framework

It would be easy to argue that all aspects of the framework have some relevance to the topic of sex. I will focus here on two particular features of the framework, those to do with the G and the E. Looking first at the G, I cannot emphasise too strongly the generational changes that are occurring where sexual behaviour is concerned. Here is an amazing statistic. Teenage pregnancy rates have fallen in a dramatic fashion since the 1990s. For the 15- to 17-year-olds, the rates in England and Wales fell by 60 per cent between 1990 and 2016. For the under-15s the change has been even more dramatic. In England and Wales in 1990 there were 8,500 pregnancies in this age group, whereas in 2016 this number was 2,000. There are many possible explanations for this change, but the most likely appears to be that teenagers are simply having less sex. Furthermore, this is a trend that is true across Western Europe and North America. It is not restricted to the UK only.

In addition to the changes that seem to be happening in levels of sexual behaviour, the opportunities created by the digital world have led to changes in values and attitudes as well as to alterations in behaviour. Sexual behaviour is initiated, explored, negotiated, and experienced in a manner that is completely new to generations of adults who grew up before the 1990s. It is hard for parents and carers to keep in mind that their own beliefs and opinions about what is appropriate and healthy are not the same as the opinions and attitudes of young people. Nowhere is the G for generation gap more relevant and important than in the sphere of sexual behaviour.

Where E for emotion is concerned, this too can be seen to be an element of the framework which applies to the sexual behaviour of young people. Sex is something that has always aroused strong feelings among the adults who watch and worry. However, today, partly because of the generational differences outlined above, new feelings come into play. Sexual behaviour may seem even more puzzling for adults today, creating more anxiety. Sexual behaviour in the digital world may make parents feel even more excluded, even more at a loss as to how to respond and play a role as a supportive adult. As I have argued in other parts of the book, the more aware parents can be of their emotions, the better they will be able to manage them.

Gender identity

There has been a remarkable shift in attitudes to gender in recent years. For centuries gender has been considered as a binary concept, in other words everyone was either male or female. Today, however, there is a more flexible approach, with many individuals questioning the gender that was assigned to them at birth. The trans movement has become more visible, with a number of young people believing that they can change gender or remain what is known as "gender neutral". For the first time it is now possible to consider three genders rather than two.

There has been marked social change since the 1970s. At that time parents were encouraged to avoid stereotyping. Toys and books that were identified as specifically female or male were criticised, and girls in particular were praised if they behaved as tomboys. Things changed in the 1990s. Pink became popular, and girls were able to enjoy "girly" books and toys. Today, however, there is a trend to avoid identifying children by their gender.

For many parents this can be a puzzling experience. The word "trans" is used to describe young people who are unsure of their gender, or who feel that the gender they were assigned at birth does not match their sense of self. These young people argue that the idea of there being only two genders (the "gender binary") is deeply embedded in society, but that this attitude discriminates against those who are unsure of their gender.

What can you as a parent do if you have a teenager who believes he or she is trans? As with other examples of teenage behaviour that are unexpected or out of the mainstream, the first thing to remember is not to over-react. Do not rush into a response, but try and delay any reaction until you learn more. Inform yourself about what this generation of young people thinks about gender. Try and listen to what your teenager has to say without rushing to judgement. Above all be supportive. Teenagers need to know that they are loved, whatever choice they make about their gender.

Early sexual relationships

Young people's sexual relationships develop in a wider context. They are, of course, influenced by what they see around them in the family and neighbourhood, as well as by what they experience through the digital world. Attitudes and values relating to sex are constantly changing, and as I have said, these will certainly be different from those that were in place when parents themselves were growing up.

One major difference between the experiences of teenagers today and those of a previous generation has to do with the role of technology and the digital world. I will be dealing with this topic in detail in Chapter 12. For the present, however, it is important to note that young people's lives have been changed dramatically by technology, as is illustrated in the section on Digital Romance in this chapter.

As far as parents are concerned, there are many possible causes of anxiety in relation to teenage sexuality. Quite apart from the challenges posed by the internet, there are other worries, such as:

- the pressure on teenagers to have sex early,
- the effect of alcohol or drugs on sexual behaviour,
- the sexually explicit content of games, films, TV shows, and social media.

In thinking about early sexual relationships all these have to be taken into account. Boys and girls are growing up in a very sexualised world, and this will inevitably affect their attitudes and their behaviour. It is important to remember that there are many stages involved in learning about sex. Most teenagers explore sex in tentative or explorative ways, either on-line or in person, before they engage in actual sexual intercourse.

One of the questions often asked by teenagers is: "When will I be ready to have sex?". This is not an easy question for parents to address honestly. The parent's own values about sex, as well as worries about the young person's safety and welfare may get in the way of a helpful answer. What the teenager needs most is a non-judgemental answer, but one that is realistic about the risks of having a sexual relationship at a young age.

One of the most helpful ways forward is to outline a set of questions that the young person can ask themselves. If the answer to any of these questions is no, then the teenager is not ready to have a sexual relationship. Here are the questions:

- Are you sure you can trust the other person?
- Do you actually feel ready yourself? If the other person is putting pressure on you, then you are not ready.
- Can you discuss and decide about contraception together?
- Have you thought about the emotions that may be created after having sex?
- Are you absolutely sure that you and your partner will be protected against pregnancy and sexually transmitted infections?

Of course this all sounds very rational, and as we all know, sex is hardly a rational subject! A first sexual experience may take place at a party when everyone has had too much to drink, and there is no preparation beforehand. Research on the attitudes and fears of teenage girls show that some feel they have to have sex to hold on to a boyfriend. Others feel under pressure because it appears as if all their friends are already doing it. As for boys, having sex may be more to do with reputation among male peers than with establishing a long-term relationship.

Although young people may give the impression that they are not influenced by their parents, in fact the opposite is true. In areas of morality and values, particularly where these are to do with relationships, research shows clearly that teenagers are very much influenced and affected by their parents. In addition, while talking is important, in areas like this it is behaviour that carries just as much weight. Teenagers will be intensely aware of how their parents behave in intimate relationships. It does not matter whether this is with a husband or wife, or with a new partner. What you do will matter just as much as what you say!

To conclude this section, I will summarise two pieces of important research. First, while it is generally believed that the majority of teenagers will have had sex by the age of 16, this is not the case. The evidence is clear that in the UK only a third of those in this age group are sexually active. Thus two out of every three 16-year-olds will not have had sex. The average age for first sex is 18, not 15 or 16. This should be reassuring to those teenagers who feel that they are the only ones who are not yet sexually active.

Second, studies show that the more open discussion there is between parents and teenagers, the more likely young people are to delay before they start to have sex. In other words, the more opportunities there are for parents and young people to talk about the various issues surrounding sexual health, the more careful teenagers are likely to be. It has been argued that if adults mention sex, then young people will want to go out and try it. However, there is no evidence to support this. In families in which these things can be discussed, teenagers will be more likely to take a responsible attitude to sex.

Digital romance

We are all aware that the digital world makes possible various types of behaviour associated with sex, such as viewing pornography or sexting. By and large these behaviours are ones that raise anxiety among adults. Parents worry about how to restrict or prevent these behaviours, and they encourage a negative view of what happens in the digital world. I will be discussing some of these threats in Chapter 12.

The adult world is less aware of the ways in which young people use the digital world to pursue romantic experiences. In 2017 an important research project was published, entitled *Digital romance*. This was carried out by two reputable organisations, and provided a valuable insight into the way in which romantic and sexual relationships have been altered and enhanced by the internet.

By and large the overall picture that emerges from this study is a positive one. Those who took part, ranging in age from 14 to 25, viewed the opportunities afforded by the on-line world as providing a rich experience of intimate relationships. This was illustrated through experiences of meeting partners on-line, of being able to flirt without embarrassment, of being intimate without being together, and most importantly being able to stay in touch at all times. Some in the study reported almost constant messaging when they felt they were in love.

The less positive aspects of the digital world included feeling pressured to do things or be intimate when that felt uncomfortable; 25 per cent of girls and 10 per cent of boys reported having this experience. Break-ups also happened on-line, and these can be painful and distressing. Again this was rare, but when it did happen it represented a negative use of the digital world. There were also a few reports of people entering an on-line relationship when the other person turned out to be a much older adult.

The key message from this research is that digital romance does not take over from face-to-face relationships. Rather the opportunities of the digital world mostly enhance relationships, and enable people to have a wider range of intimate experiences. For the minority who did have negative experiences they felt these could have happened in a face-to-face relationship, and they did not attach blame to the on-line world. However, they did want more education in digital literacy, which they believed was poorly delivered and did not get the attention it deserved in schools.

Contraception

The topic of contraception represents a good example of the important role that a parent can play, as well as the pitfalls and problems that can exist. Here is one young person talking about her experiences.

> I remember when I wanted to go on the pill, it took me weeks and weeks to ask my Mum. I remember I was like waiting for the right moment for weeks, like, and then she just said: "Yeah, ok, I'll come down to the clinic with you". And I was going "Aaaaargh!" I had to wait until we went on holiday, and my Mum had had a few drinks to eventually ask her, but she was fine about it. It was so embarrassing!
>
> (18-year-old young woman)

Parents may fear that helping with contraceptive advice is to intrude on something private, or is simply impossible to talk about. In so many families it is experienced as embarrassing, but as the quote above shows, once it is out in the open, it will be fine. Of course much depends on how the subject is approached.

If the parent tries to take over, treating the teenager like an irresponsible child, it will not go down too well! If the parent treads cautiously, offering advice and support when and if the young person wants it, then this is likely to be more acceptable.

The question of contraception is a difficult one for young people, and they do need advice to get it right. There will be different issues for different couples, but there are some common questions which are relevant for most people. These include finding the right type of pill, learning about the long-term effects of the oral contraceptive, and knowing about other methods, such as barrier methods of contraception. Parents and teenagers should also know about emergency contraception (sometimes called the "morning-after" pill) just in case it is ever needed.

What about differences between boys and girls? The role of parents with boys may appear less obvious, but it is just as important. Indeed most of the things that apply to girls are just as true with boys. Parents need to make sure boys have the right information about contraception and about sexually transmitted infections. Boys who may become sexually active need to have access to condoms, and parents can check that this is the case.

Adults in the family need to be sensitive, and to be respectful of the young person's privacy. However, they can also make it clear that they are available to offer support when needed. Boys may be more reticent than girls in talking about emotive or embarrassing topics. However, it is surprising how often boys will find a reason to share things, as long as they feel their views will be treated with respect.

Gay, lesbian, and bi-sexual relationships

Estimates of the number of people who are gay, lesbian, or bi-sexual vary considerably. It is generally believed that there are approximately one in 10 people in the population who are gay, lesbian, or bi-sexual, although there are probably many more who have had both homosexual and heterosexual experiences. There is also a great variation in the age at which individuals realise that they may not be heterosexual. Some are aware from late childhood, whereas others are not sure about their sexual orientation until late adolescence or into the adult years.

In spite of great changes in attitudes to gay and lesbian sexuality over the past 20 or 30 years, there still remains a significant degree of prejudice and misunderstanding. Teenagers who think they may be gay, lesbian, or bi-sexual struggle to find support, and often feel isolated and alone. What is known as homophobic bullying (where gay, lesbian, or bi-sexual individuals are targets of bullying) is still a problem in schools and workplaces. Organisations that work with gay, lesbian, and bi-sexual young people report higher levels of mental health problems than are seen in the population at large.

In the context of the family, one of the hardest things is for someone to tell their parents that they are gay, lesbian, or bi-sexual.

> When I was 15 I started going to gay pubs and everything, which you shouldn't do at that age, but it's quite an awful age and I successfully managed to go out for 2 years until I was 17. It got to a point where I was lying about everything I did, in the family I was lying, and I just got fed up with it. So I just came out with it one night. It always comes out like one big thing. When I told my Dad he was in bed at the time, and I sat on the end of the bed and I said: "I'm gay". I just watched the colour drain out of his face. It was OK to start off with, but when he spoke to my Mum she was really upset about it. I'd sort of led them on, letting them think I had a girlfriend and this and that. That's why they never had any idea at all. It was round about Christmas last year, and it ruined their Christmas, don't know about mine!
>
> (19-year-old man)

Parents may very well be shocked or upset to discover that their son is gay or their daughter is lesbian. The sexuality of our children does arouse complicated feelings, and this is especially so when we discover they are "different" from ourselves. Parents will need time to get used to such things. It is worth remembering that, after a period of adjustment, many parents come to be proud of their gay son or lesbian daughter. They may come to recognise that a lifestyle that is different from their own can be a fulfilling and satisfying one. Here is a young lesbian woman giving her advice:

> Parents should not give an immediate reaction, because immediate reactions hurt so much. Because it's taken that child so much courage to actually say something. So just think about what you are saying, and go away and think about it. Think about your priorities and if you love that child more than you hate their sexuality. I think you need a lot of time to think.
>
> (17-year-old young woman)

Unless parents have already had some inkling of the possibility, it can be very hard indeed to come to terms with this situation. Taking time to respond might sound like a good strategy, but it will not be easy to put into practice. Many parents report shock and disbelief. Some say that they feel guilty, asking themselves where they went wrong. Others shut their eyes and hope the situation will go away. None of these reactions are helpful. So what can be done?

- Recognise that this is not the end of the world! Your son or daughter is still the same person. He or she has not become someone different just because they have told you about their sexual orientation. This is not the end of the world, rather it is the beginning of a more open and honest relationship between you.
- Reassure your son or daughter that you still love them. They need your support and love more than ever at this time. The young person will be experiencing acute feelings of uncertainty, anxiety, and lack of confidence about themselves. They need to know that you are there for them.
- Try to be as well-informed as possible. You may well need someone to talk to, to help you sort out your reaction. Do not be afraid to seek advice, and do find someone who can give a helpful perspective on the situation.
- If this is appropriate, ask to meet your son or daughter's partner. This may not be easy, but it can send a powerful signal that you are not closing the door. If you can welcome the person who is

special to your son or daughter into your home, this will reflect your willingness to accept who they are. You will have worries and fears, but it will be seen by your son or daughter as a huge step towards acceptance and reconciliation.

Sex and the law

There are a number of ways in which the laws concerning sexual behaviour are relevant to young people. There are many areas of confusion, and it is important for parents and young people to have a certain level of knowledge about these matters. In this section I will deal with three issues:

- the age of consent,
- confidentiality in medical consultations,
- sexual abuse and exploitation.

As far as the age of consent is concerned, the law protects children until they are considered old enough to make their own decisions about sex. This age is known as the age of consent. If a man or boy has sex with a girl who is below the age of consent, this person is committing a criminal offence. In England, Scotland, and Wales the age of consent is 16, while in Northern Ireland it is 17, and in the Republic of Ireland it is 18. In England, Scotland, and Wales the age of consent is the same for heterosexual and homosexual relationships.

This law does not apply to women. A girl or woman cannot be prosecuted for unlawful sexual intercourse if she has sex with a boy of any age, even someone under 16. However, there are circumstances where a woman can be prosecuted for indecent sexual assault if, for example, she is a teacher or social worker in a position of trust. It is also important to note that anyone in a position of trust and over the age of 18 can be prosecuted if they engage in any sexual activity with someone under the age of 18.

It has to be acknowledged that many young people do have sexual relationships where either or both partners are under the age of 16. In such cases the young people involved do not realise they are breaking the law. It is rare for the police to interfere, except in special circumstances. This could be because a parent or carer objects to the relationship, or because a responsible adult such as a social worker considers the young person to be in "moral danger". This would apply where a young person might be involved in prostitution, or if they were considered to be at risk of sexual exploitation.

Turning now to the question of medical confidentiality, this has proved a thorny issue, and one which the law has not found easy to resolve. It should first be noted that anyone aged 16 or above has a right to confidential medical treatment. At that age parents no longer have any legal standing, and cannot insist on being involved or consulted about their daughter's or son's treatment.

The problem arises if the teenager is under the age of 16. This issue first came to prominence in the 1980s, when a parent in England took her local health authority to court. She claimed that, in giving her daughter treatment (in this case contraceptive advice) without her knowledge, the health authority had breached her parental rights. The Law Lords disagreed, arguing that in certain circumstances a young person should have the right to confidential medical treatment. These circumstances were deemed to be as follows:

- where the girl (although under 16) would understand the doctor's advice,
- where the doctor has tried, but cannot persuade the girl to inform her parents, nor is able to persuade the girl to allow him/her to inform the parents,
- where the doctor believes it's in the girl's best interests that the treatment be given, even though the parents have not been informed.

Subsequent guidelines from the Department of Health indicate that a young person of any age, whether male or female, is entitled to a confidential consultation with a doctor, provided that the above criteria are met and that the young person makes it clear that she/he does not wish the parents to be informed. However, a doctor who is unwilling to accept a request for confidentiality can refuse to continue with the consultation.

This has led to an unsatisfactory situation, as a young person has first to establish a doctor's attitude to confidentiality before knowing what to expect. Some GPs do make clear that they offer a confidential service, but this is far from universal. In practice doctors vary widely in their beliefs about confidentiality, and it is not surprising that young people are confused about the issue. If a young person does need confidential consultation it will be best to seek help from an organisation such as Brook, or attend a dedicated local sexual health service or family planning clinic.

The last topic to be covered here is sexual abuse and exploitation. While for many years this was a hidden subject, a number of high profile cases involving celebrities and broadcasters have led to a greater awareness of the problem in recent times. What areas are covered by the law here?

- Incest – a sexual relationship with a close relative is treated as a criminal act against the child or young person.
- Sexual intercourse or any other form of sexual intimacy by an adult who is in a position of trust (e.g. a teacher) with someone under the age of 18 is an offence against the young person and can lead to prosecution.
- Grooming became a criminal offence in the UK in 2003. Grooming is any attempt by an adult to entice, either on the internet or in person, a child or young person to meet them for sexual activity.
- Peer-on-peer sexual violence is an offence.
- Sexual exploitation, including trafficking for sexual purposes, involving young people in pornography, and other similar activities are all criminal offences.

There has been much publicity given to the question of safety on the internet, and the possibility of a young person being groomed or getting involved with a predator through a website or chat room. This is a worrying subject for parents, but it has to be seen in the wider context of the internet and its role in the lives of young people. I will have more to say about this in Chapter 12 when I discuss the different ways young people engage with the digital world.

As far as sexual abuse is concerned, it may be hard for an adult to believe that someone they know has been sexually abusing a young person. This can mean that the honesty of the child or young person is doubted by those around them. If you are in this situation remember that it is not easy to make up a story about sexual abuse. It is highly likely that what you are hearing is the truth.

It is sometimes believed that, so long as the actual abuse can be prevented from happening again, the whole matter is best forgotten. However, adults who abuse children or young people may be unable to stop, and may well go on to abuse others. Furthermore, the child or young person will need help to undo the damaging effects of the abuse once it has occurred.

If you suspect a child or young person you know is being sexually abused you have a responsibility to talk about it – however hard or disagreeable this may be. Do seek professional help. If something can be done you will be protecting not just the young person you know, but possibly many others as well.

The fears and anxieties of teenagers

I will end this chapter by looking at some common fears and worries of both parents and teenagers. We can start by considering the fears of teenagers.

- My body is not normal.
  First, everyone is different. There is no such thing as normal where bodies are concerned. Everyone develops at a different rate, and no two people are the same. The second point to note is that the way we develop during puberty has no relation to how we are as mature adults. Whether the teenager is slow or fast in terms of development during puberty will be forgotten within a few years. It may seem very important at the time for a teenager to be in step with his or her friends, but this will become irrelevant by the age of 16 or 17.
- Do I think about sex too much?
  Many young people find that, as they move into adolescence, the subject of sex begins to dominate their thoughts. As with everything to do with sex, there are great differences between individuals. Some young people may spend a lot of time having daydreams or fantasies about sex. They may lie in bed thinking about sex, they may masturbate, or they may seek out sexual material in books or on the internet. On the other hand there may be others of the same age who do none of these things. In the majority of cases it can be stated that there is no such thing as thinking about sex too much. (The only exception to this would be a situation where a young person becomes obsessively pre-occupied with sex, for example with pornography on the internet). We all have different levels of sexual need, and different levels of arousal. Each of us has to find healthy and satisfying outlets for our sexual desires.
- Should I have done "it" by now?
  Young people come under considerable pressure to become sexually active. This pressure comes not only from the peer group, but from the media and from society in general. There is also much exaggeration, by both girls and boys, about the extent of their sexual experience. As I have already noted, there are a number of things parents can do to help teenagers resist peer

99

pressure and make responsible decisions for themselves. One key thing is to make sure young people have good information about sexual health, and another is to be available to offer support at times when it is most needed.

- Am I too easily aroused?/Am I too frigid?
It is entirely understandable that the question of sexual arousal should become a matter of concern at this age. For both boys and girls sexual experience is tied up with some many other aspects of identity. Will I be attractive to someone else? Will I be able to satisfy someone else? How will I perform when I first have sex with someone? All these anxieties and many others are an inevitable part of growing up and learning about relationships. These may be topics that are very difficult to discuss. However, for parents it is important to remember how much uncertainty and lack of confidence will be experienced by a teenager at this time.

- Am I gay, lesbian, or straight?
While some teenagers may be quite sure of their sexual orientation from an early age, many others will go through a stage of uncertainty and questioning. As I have noted, issues to do with identity are central during these years. Being clear about one's sexual orientation is an extremely important element in the overall search for a stable identity. For those who are not sure, this question can come to dominate their thoughts and anxieties. It is a great shame that in our society we provide so few opportunities for these matters to be discussed. Any support that can be given by parents in such situations can make all the difference.

The fears and anxieties of parents

- Sex is too embarrassing to discuss.
This is a major concern of parents. It is embarrassing to talk about sex with your children. Most people experience this, so you can be sure you are not alone! One possible approach is to let the young person know that you think it is important to talk, but that you feel it is embarrassing. Saying that may be enough to get you started. You may both laugh, and then it will possible to start on at least some aspect of the subject. One mother put it like this:

> Well, I'd say, no matter how hard it is, grit your teeth, giggle, and get it out. Get it out of your mouth, because

100

once you've got it out the first time, it will be easier. All I can say is take a deep breath and have a go. Speaking about it, talking about it, just admitting that it is difficult. That is all that you need, really.

(Mother of two daughters)

- I want to talk, but my teenager avoids the subject.
  This situation occurs most often because the subject is tackled in the wrong way. Don't force the issue. Choose a moment when your teenager wants to talk. Start by letting them set the agenda. Use a TV programme or other event to open a discussion. Try to avoid being judgemental or moralistic about sex. Above all, show that you are willing to listen. A good listener is the best communicator.

- I am worried that if we do talk, we will end up having a row.
  This is another common worry. You may find that you and your teenager disagree, but this does not mean you will have a violent row. Try to accept each other's differences. If you can do this, you will be accepting that your son or daughter is an individual in their own right.

- I am worried that my teenager will be subjected to pressure from unsuitable friends.
  Peer pressure is a powerful force which operates among all of us. However, this may have more impact for teenagers because of the importance of friends during these years. I will have more to say about the role of friends in the next chapter. For the present it is worth noting that some young people are more able to resist peer pressure than others, and parents can be helpful here. If possible try not to criticise your teenager's friends, or exclude them from your home. The more they are part of your life, the more influence you will have, and the more chance you will have of keeping an eye on what's going on.

- Not under my roof!
  There is an excellent book with this title, written by Amy Schalet, an American sociologist. She studied parents' reactions to their teenagers having sex in the family home. This is a very difficult issue, and one with which many parents struggle. Of course much depends on the age and maturity of the young person. However, there are thorny questions to be addressed here.

  On the one hand saying yes implies trust and respect for the young person. In addition, it means you can get to know the boyfriend or girlfriend, and can keep in touch with how things are going. It also ensures that the teenager is having sex in a comfortable and protected place, thus making it more likely that a safe contraceptive method will be used.

On the other hand you may feel that if you say yes, you are condoning teenage sex. If there are younger siblings in the house you may want to protect them, and knowing that your teenager is having sex under your roof may make you feel awkward and uncomfortable.

In the end all families have to weigh up their beliefs and feelings, and take into account the individual circumstances. To my mind it is the point about protection that tips the balance. As parents we do have a responsibility to assist young people in every way to protect themselves against risk. Above all we want them to be safe, and they are more likely to be safe in their own home than anywhere else.

Conclusion

This is a good point on which to conclude the chapter. The sexual behaviour of our sons and daughters will pose challenges for us as parents. We will almost certainly have different attitudes to sex, and there will be tricky choices and decisions to be made. To maintain good relationships it may be necessary to accept things that we do not feel happy about. One of the fathers we interviewed expressed it well when he pointed out that there is a fine line between acceptance and approval.

> I feel that no matter how much you disapprove of the youngster's sexual attitudes, the chances are that they are going to do it anyway, and you have to decide whether you are going to bridge that gap and try to understand what they do, or risk them deceiving you. So you may just have to look away and accept what you don't approve of. And there is a fine line between acceptance and approval.
>
> (Father of two daughters)

11

FRIENDS AND THE PEER GROUP

The social life of the teenager can be all consuming. If you imagine your son or daughter in class at school, you may expect that he or she is concentrating on maths or history. Of course this is also what the teacher hopes. It is a good guess, however, that for a significant amount of time teenagers will be thinking about their social life.

Your teenager will be thinking about a post on a social media site, why one person sent a photo to another, what is going to happen on the weekend, and so on. These matters are pre-occupying for teenagers, and in this chapter I will be exploring why friends, the peer group, and social life matter so much to young people.

It will be obvious that smart phones and the internet have led to greatly increased communication between young people. This will be discussed in greater detail in the next chapter. For the moment, however, it is important to note that the arrival of technology has altered the social world of most teenagers. On the one hand communication between friends has become so much easier, while on the other it can be argued that digital technology has led to communication itself becoming a central feature of friendship at this age.

The STAGE framework

You will have noticed that at the beginning of each chapter I am emphasising how the STAGE framework applies to the particular topic being discussed. Where friends and the peer group are concerned, the most obvious relevance of the framework comes from the S, standing for Significance. Why is this? As I noted in Chapter 4, this is the time when adults start to feel left out. Young people may give the impression that they prefer to talk to their friends rather than to their parents. The cosy relationship which existed between parent and child is no longer there. Parents begin to feel that they are less important than they were.

Teenagers want to share their experiences with friends rather than with parents. They give the impression that they are no longer interested in what the parent has to say. They may even be pushing the adults away, shutting the bedroom door and putting up a large PRIVATE sign outside. It is for this reason that the S for Significance is so important. Parents do matter. They matter just as much as they did during childhood. The role of a parent may change, but they still have a critical role to play. In this chapter, I will consider the role of parents where friends and the peer group come to play a large part in the life of the teenager.

In this chapter I will cover the following topics:

* why friends are important during the teenage years
* the wider peer group
* whether parents or friends are more influential
* unsuitable friends
* bullying, rejection, and isolation.

Why friends are important

Friends are important in childhood, but they come to play a far more significant role as the teenage years begin. Why should this be so? There are probably three main reasons why friends become so important in adolescence.

The first reason has to do with the changing relationship with parents. The teenage years are a time when young people are starting to establish their identity as separate from the family. They are beginning to look for more independence, and to do this they may need to create a bit of distance between themselves and their parents.

Second, there is a lot of insecurity and uncertainty during the early adolescent years, and this makes individuals feel more vulnerable. The young person is dealing not only with the physical changes of puberty, but also the social and emotional changes that happen as well. We all need more support when we feel vulnerable, and at this time young people turn to their friends for some elements of this support.

The third reason is linked to the fact that the adolescent years are a time of identity development. During this time young people are finding out what sort of people they are, and who they want to be. As the young woman in this quote indicates, it is through friends as much as anything else that this process of identity development can take place.

> Friends are definitely important in giving you more confidence and feeling sort of secure and safe. And sort of they're stability. I mean I've had some bad experiences with best friends, and when it all falls apart it's a horrible experience to have to go through, but when you have a lot of good friends around you, you just feel secure. Like they wouldn't really care what you came in looking like, they'd still be your friends. And also for discovering new things, and finding out new things. They can open you up to new experiences, whether it's where to shop, or going out, or stuff like that. And new music that you get to hear, it all helps with finding your identity.
>
> (16-year-old girl)

In research on friendship during this stage it has been suggested that friends have a number of functions for teenagers. These functions include:

- companionship (someone to do things with),
- a reliable alliance (someone to be on your side),
- help (assistance in time of need),
- intimacy (someone to share things with),
- self-validation (someone to confirm that you are ok, that you are someone who can make friends, someone who is liked by others),
- emotional security (someone to prop you up when you feel vulnerable).

It will be apparent that these are all very important functions. However, parents should not feel that this diminishes their role. What is happening is that both parents and friends have their part to play. In the best of circumstances these two sources of support work together for the good of the teenager. I will talk more about the different roles of each in a moment.

People sometimes ask what happens if a teenager does not have any friends. It is reassuring to know that a proportion of teenagers manage quite well without close friends. Nonetheless there are some things to bear in mind. Quite often teenagers who do not have friends will have someone or something that compensates. For example the teenager may be close to a sibling, or to another relative such as a cousin. Alternatively, the young person will find a hobby or interest that claims their attention, and in which they can become closely involved.

For parents it is essential not to panic or worry too much. Everyone is different, and some do not need friends as much as others. The key thing is for the parent to be able to support the teenager. Young people should be enabled to enjoy their friends if that is what they want, or encouraged with any other pursuits or interests that they have if these do not include friends.

The wider peer group

For parents the idea of peer pressure is a worrying notion. We do not want our daughters or sons to be influenced by others, especially when that influence is seen to be negative. Phrases such as "getting in with the wrong crowd" and "being led astray" represent the fears that many parents have at one time or another about their teenagers.

As one mother put it:

> Certainly my experience of peer group pressure was of being very stressed, and I see my daughter going though that now. How to keep friends but say what she thinks about things, and what she feels, without being frightened that her friends are not going to want to know her. So standing up for herself under pressure is a big difficulty.
>
> (Mother of one daughter and two sons)

While young people can choose their friends (to some extent at least), they cannot choose the larger peer group. However, the move to secondary school brings teenagers into contact with this wider group, and they have to learn how to manage the pressures that stem from it. Some individuals are more open to influence than others. Research shows that age and personality both make a difference. The older the teenager, the more likely she or he is to be able to stand up to the crowd. However, there are also big differences between individuals – some teenagers are more likely to conform to peer group pressure than others.

There are two major reasons why being accepted by the wider peer group is important. In the first place popularity matters – we all want to be popular, and acceptance by the peer group is a measure of popularity. At no time is this more important than during the teenage years. Second, the peer group offers a means of working out what sort of a person you are. The crowd you belong to will help you establish what activities you like, and what suits you best.

> I'm kind of changing at the moment, like with the friends I prefer to be with, and I'm still trying to work it out. It's like certain groups aren't very popular, but with their group they are, and then there's people in the middle that are good friends with the lower people, and then there's the really popular people who are friends with everyone. I think I'm sort of in the middle but I'm still like edging my way round.
>
> (15-year-old girl)

Peer pressure is a fact of life – we all experience it. However, this is more likely to play a part in the lives of teenagers than in other age groups because the peer group is especially important at this time.

There is one clear conclusion from all the research on peer group influence:

- The more involved and supportive the family is, the fewer opportunities there will be for the peer group to exercise a negative influence on teenage behaviour.

If the family is not available to provide the necessary support, there is a gap, and it is this gap or vacuum which is filled by the peer group. Young people need support, and they need a sense of belonging. If the family does not fulfil this function, then the peer group can have a significant influence. Support from the family will provide a buffer against excessive peer group pressure.

In conclusion, it is important to say that all teenagers, no matter how supportive their families are, will experience peer pressure. They will need help and support to be able to manage this pressure. This leads me on neatly to the next section.

Do parents or peers have more influence?

This question is one that has dominated research on parents and teenagers, and there are numerous studies on this issue. To put it in a nutshell, the results show that it is a misleading question. The answer is not either/or, the answer is both. We cannot say that either parents or peers are more influential. The correct answer is that both play different roles. Both are important in different ways.

PART II

This 15-year-old boy was asked whether he would be more influenced by his parents or his friends:

> I'd probably try and find somewhere in the middle rather
> than telling either of them no, so they'd both be sort of
> happy. Rather than, because I wouldn't want to annoy my
> parents because you're sort in the same house, but I wouldn't
> want to lose my friends either. But it depends on what it is.
> I'd probably end up doing what my parents want, because
> they sort of know me more than my friends, but if my friends
> are saying something, like wanting to do something that is
> really fun, I would think ... but it does depend on what it is,
> doesn't it?

In a recent study young people were asked who they would go to for
advice on different issues. The results illustrated how both parents and
peers play different roles. When asked who they would talk to about
school problems or health issues, over 70 per cent said they would go
to their parents, and less than 30 per cent mentioned their friends. On
the other hand, when asked who they would go to to discuss boyfriend
or girlfriend problems, nearly 65 per cent said they would talk to their
friends, and only 35 per cent said they would talk to their parents.

Thus it can be seen that individual teenagers differ in who they
prefer to talk to, but also the topic itself makes a difference. In the
majority of cases parents are seen as being the ones to turn to when it
comes to education, careers, and jobs, health matters, money, and
questions of morality. Where it is a question of social issues, where
there are concerns about intimate relationships, and where such
things as clothes, music, and leisure are discussed, then friends
become more important.

Two more points are worth making. Many teenagers say that they
feel more comfortable talking to friends rather than to parents. One
of the reasons for this is that friends respond differently. Friends
won't give you a lecture, and they won't criticise you. Friends will be
more accepting, and they will be more neutral and objective when
asked for advice on a difficult issue. They will listen, rather than talk
at you. This is something parents do need to bear in mind.

The second point to make is that parents and friends are not separate, but they are both part of the same system. What teenagers bring
to their friendships will be influenced by what they have learnt in the
home. They will be influenced by their parents' own social relationships. Most importantly, the way the parents respond to the teenager's

friends will make a difference in the amount of influence these friends will have. The more parents get to know their teenager's friends, and the more these friends can be welcomed into the home, the more influence the parents will retain.

Unsuitable friends

> We had a terrible time with our daughter. One moment she was going to school, quite normal, healthy, an intelligent girl, and the next minute she had changed completely. She met up with this boy, and we found out they were playing truant. Smoking pot apparently. She's an intelligent girl, but she went with this bloke who had no interest in school. She became like him, she talked and acted like him. We didn't like the boy, but we thought the more we said about him, the more it would draw her to him.
>
> (Father of three teenagers)

This sort of situation is every parent's nightmare. This example is an extreme one, but it does illustrate the dilemma faced by parents if their teenager does start to go around with friends who, for whatever reason, are considered unsuitable. In such situations parents will be faced with a choice. On the one hand they can make plain their dislike of the particular individual or individuals, and risk damaging the relationship with the teenager. On the other hand they can swallow their personal disapproval, and hope that the relationship will not last too long. However, difficult the circumstances are, the following things are worth remembering.

- Don't expect your teenager to have the same sort of friends as you do yourself.
  You do not expect your teenager to like all your friends – after all, why should they? Perhaps what looks to you like an unsuitable friendship or relationship is not really unsuitable, it just involves people you don't particularly like. You may not care much for the particular individual or individuals, but your teenager has to make her/his own choices, and they may not be your own choices.
- Teenagers won't always get it right.
  Part of the growing up process is bound to involve making some bad choices. The teenager has to learn, and part of this may involve having a few friendships that don't work out. The role of

the parent is not to criticise, but to provide support and the opportunity to reflect on which friendships are best for that particular young person.

• Do you really want your teenager to get involved with people away from home, where you will have no way of knowing what is going on?

If you do feel so strongly that you want to let your son or daughter know about your feelings, it is important to consider the implications of this decision. If you fall out over this, it may be that your teenager will be spending time away from home, excluding you from his/her life with a partner or with friends. There will be no opportunity for the teenager to compare your values with those of their peer group.

If you can keep your opinions to yourself for a while, there will be more chance of remaining in touch, and you are likely to have more influence. If you make this a focus of conflict between you, your son or daughter will have little choice but to keep the relationship going – as a matter of pride if for no other reason.

Rejection, isolation, and bullying

Earlier in the chapter I talked about those who go through the teenage years without friends. Some cope well with this situation, either finding support from people in the family, or getting immersed in an activity or a hobby that takes the place of friendship.

Of course this is not always the case. Some experience rejection from the peer group because of their own aggressive or inappropriate behaviour. Others may find themselves isolated because of poor social skills or extreme shyness. A third group may struggle because of bullying. All these situations are painful, both for the young person and for the parents who may have to watch from the sidelines.

Looking first at those who are isolated, some may have had earlier problems with friendships at the primary school stage, while others may find the start of adolescence especially difficult. Moving from a small informal group in primary school to a much larger school environment can be a daunting experience. Many schools now provide some preparation for the transition from primary to secondary education, and this can help with the adjustment that is necessary to cope with larger friendship groups.

Those who experience rejection will have a different sort of social problem. They may try to make friends, but find themselves being rebuffed by the group. This will be because of behaviour that is irritating or unwelcome, or because of behaviour that does not fit with the social expectations of the others.

It is important to note that social skills can be learnt. It is possible, for example, to help an extremely shy teenager become more confident. It is also possible to help those who have an aggressive approach to learn to moderate their behaviour when in social situations. It may be worth seeking professional help from a school counsellor or someone similar if your teenager is experiencing problems like this.

Both isolated and rejected teenagers can find themselves the target of bullying, and I will now move on to this topic. I will discuss cyberbullying in a section in Chapter 12 which deals with teenagers and technology.

Here is one father's story about his son who was bullied at school.

My wife thought there was something going on for quite a while. I'm not as good at it as she is, but she picked up on something, we were asking if everything was alright for quite a while but he never said anything. In the end he just came out with it, it was like he'd been bottling up for so long that it all exploded out one day. We'd had an argument one day about something, I can't remember what, and then it all came out, what had been done and it was just shocking. It was like my stomach just dropped out, and it was this sense of powerlessness and "What can I do?" "How can I stop this?". The worst thing was that he didn't want us to help. I said I'd be at the school the next day, but he flat out wouldn't let us go.

(What did you do?) We didn't let him go to school the next day. And the next day after that. But we had to sort it out with the school, so my wife contacted the school, even though he had said no, and we got in contact with the head of year, and told her what was happening. They said they were aware of this group of kids, and in a way that was better and worse. Because on the one hand it was like "how can you have known about these problems and let it go on?" but then in some way it was like at least they knew and they'll take it seriously.

We made an appointment to see the head of year after school, so that no one would know that we had done it, and made a plan of what we would do. They have been really good actually. They called the main ones in, not with us there, and didn't tell them who had been informing the school, but they told them that they had become aware that there were some issues and that it was not going to be tolerated.

(Did this help?) Well, yes and no. The direct bullying has stopped, but teenagers are pack animals, and if you're a teenager you don't want to get in trouble, you want to look after yourself. So if someone has been bullied they're weak in other people's eyes, and being associated with them is only going to mean you're going to be a target too. My son has lost some of his friends through it, not all, it's not like he's been abandoned, but he knows no one is going to stick up for him.

(How has it affected him?) Well it's just one more stress, isn't it? You can tell he's got a front, he's embarrassed by it and so there's this front where everything is fine, it didn't matter, it wasn't anything. Like he would never bring it up, it's like the elephant in the room, we would never mention it because it would make him uncomfortable to talk about it.

His confidence has taken a knock, and it's all so meaningless and cruel. My son has red hair, and he's not big for his age, he's a classic target, and it just makes me so angry. It must be really hard when you're a teenager and you're trying to turn yourself into someone and then some little bastard comes along and wrecks what you've put together. I can't imagine the hurt.

I tell this story at length because there is so much in here that may be helpful for parents. Bullying can be a major worry for parents, so what lessons can be drawn from this?

In the first place it is obvious that you need to keep an eye on the moods and behaviour of your teenager. If there are changes that do not make sense, or if behaviour alters in way that is not easily explained, then be alert to any signs of bullying. The classic signs include:

- unwillingness to go to school,
- taking a different route home from school,
- personal possessions and/or clothes missing or damaged,
- any injuries or marks on the body that are not easily explained,
- persistent low mood, or irritability,

- loss of friendships,
- deterioration in school performance without reason.

All schools are required to have an anti-bullying policy, and parents have a right to know what that is. You can make it your business to find out, and to ensure that the school is operating the stated policy. If you do not feel supported by the teaching staff, you can ask other parents to help you.

The most important thing will be to open a discussion with your teenager about the problem. Seek to find out who the young person would prefer to talk to. There may be a school counsellor, year head, or personal tutor who will be someone who is easy to talk to. Try to follow the wishes of your teenager. However, as the story above illustrates, even though this boy did not want his parents to intervene, they did so. This is always a dilemma for parents, but in this case you will probably judge that they did the right thing.

Bullying is a serious problem. It must never go unchallenged. Although it may sometimes appear as if there is not much that parents can do, as the story above shows, parents can make a difference. It is often the case that the teenager will not want anyone to know about the problem. Parents need to show sensitivity, and if possible to find a way of proceeding that is acceptable to the young person. However, the bottom line is that bullying cannot be allowed to continue. If it is necessary, parents must intervene to protect their son or daughter.

Conclusion

To conclude this chapter I will suggest some top tips about teenagers and their friends.

- For teenagers, friends play an important and valuable role. In the great majority of cases friends have a positive rather than a negative impact on social development. Friendships should be encouraged and supported.
- It is important for parents to get to know their teenager's friends. The more contact there is between parents and friends, the more likely it is that parents will be able to provide support when necessary.
- Parents should avoid criticising their teenager's friends. This will only create distance between parent and teenager, and reduce the opportunity for parental influence and support.

- Peer pressure will have an impact on a teenager's life. However, the more support there is at home, the more likely it is that the teenager will be able to stand up to this pressure and learn to make decisions for themselves.
- If there are serious problems such as bullying or isolation from the peer group, parents should not sit back. There will be actions that can be taken. Parents may need help or advice about how to proceed, but there will be things that parents can do to help and assist. You will find a list of resources at the end of the book.

12

THE DIGITAL WORLD

Because of computers and phones she's up till one in the morning, and having problems waking up. She's constantly tired, which makes a kid snappy, doesn't it? Her sleeping is shocking, absolutely shocking. The thing is with this blinking social media, they don't want to miss a thing, do they? I think it's quite pressurised, they've got to keep up and they have to have great photos up on there, look at me doing this! I think it's tremendous pressure on kids.

(Mother of one daughter)

Things are so much easier now. If I want to get hold of someone I will just go on my phone, and like, text or message. You sort of rely on it so much you don't even realise it. Because I lost my phone today, so I haven't got it now, and even then I was coming home from school and I felt, like, completely vulnerable, and I was just, like, I haven't got anything to sort of, have! And it's just like, what happens if I suddenly get lost, not that I would, but you know, you start to panic.

(15-year-old girl)

All our lives have been changed by new technologies, but the age group that has been at the forefront of the digital revolution is those who are now in their teens and 20s. This age group was the first to have grown up with the internet, and as a result they are very much more skilled than their parents. This has created something of a challenge for adults, and the use of digital technology by children and teenagers probably ranks as the number one topic of anxiety for parents.

It is also important to mention the extraordinary pace of change that applies to digital technology. Websites spring up overnight.

Social media are evolving all the time. New devices come on the market, and change the landscape. We cannot know what is around the corner, and so any writer must exercise caution when discussing this topic.

In this chapter I will cover the following topics:

- the opportunities offered by the internet,
- the threats of the internet: cyber-bullying, gaming, pornography, grooming and sexual harassment, and internet addiction,
- how parents can help young people stay safe on-line.

The STAGE framework

Before I move on to these topics I should note how the STAGE framework applies to the role of parents in the context of the digital world. In essence all aspects of the framework could be applied, but here I will concentrate on the A for Authority. The challenges of the digital world bring up key authority issues in the relationship between parent and teenager. How can the parent expect to exercise authority in a realm where the young person may know more than the adult? How can authority be exercised when anxieties about safety are stronger for the parent than they are for the teenager? Later in this chapter I will discuss what is known as media monitoring. Here I will argue that the best approach is one that takes the authoritative approach, an approach to parenting that I outlined in Chapter 6. Becoming overly controlling, or giving up and leaving it to the teenager are not the best approaches in this situation. Authoritative parenting can offer a way forward. There will be more about this later in the chapter.

The opportunities offered by the internet

One of the most intense debates concerning the use of digital technologies has to do with whether these are a benefit or a harmful influence on our children. On the one hand some commentators argue that too much time with a smart phone or in front of a screen damages the brain, undermines core values, harms the family, and takes away childhood innocence. I have heard journalists talking of "screenagers" or of "screen-shaped children"! On the other hand many experts point to the enormous advantages of digital technology for education and for information sharing.

Most writers take a balanced view, accepting that there are risks to young people, but stressing the positive aspects of the digital world. There are some obvious benefits of digital technologies for young people. The first point to make is that digital technologies have made keeping in touch with friends easier than ever before. If texting, messaging, emailing, using social networking sites, and using phones are all included, the potential for communication is immense.

The desire to keep in touch with friends is hardly new. In previous generations it was common for parents to complain about the constant use of the phone. Mothers and fathers would ask why it was necessary for a teenager to spend hours chatting to someone they had seen only a few minutes beforehand.

In that sense nothing has changed. What is new, however, is the ease of communication, the range of media available, and the potential to widen the communication network. Keeping in touch with others is now more like a habit, so that young people feel unsettled if they cannot access their messages and social media platforms all the time. There are many positives inherent in this world of instant communication, but there are also of course some disadvantages. I will come to these in due course.

Apart from communication, a second function of the internet for young people is that it acts as a tool for the exploration of identity. In earlier chapters I referred to the fact that the teenage years are a time of identity development. During these years young people will be trying out various selves, attempting to work out who they are and who they want to become. Both chat rooms and social networking sites allow the possibility of manipulating how the individual is presented to others. For this reason the internet provides an ideal forum for trying on different identities. This is one of the reasons that social media are so attractive to young people.

One question which has provoked heated debate relates to whether constant communication through a screen reduces face-to-face interaction. Interestingly the research shows just the opposite. Studies indicate that those who use many different digital media for communication are also good face-to-face communicators. It appears that on-line communication actually fosters closer relationships between friends, as it provides greater opportunities for intimacy and for sharing.

In addition to the benefits of communication, identity exploration, and of course instant access to banks of information, there are some other important benefits that should be mentioned.

- An opportunity for the development of social skills. There are many ways in which the use of the internet helps young people develop social skills. A good example is the use of electronic games, many of which involve groups of young people working together. In this way teenagers can learn negotiation, sharing, and joint decision-making.

- An arena for the development of autonomy. As I have noted, this is a time when opportunities for independent thought and action are so important. The internet provides many avenues where such opportunities are available. The freedom afforded by the internet may be a cause for parental anxiety, but teenagers need arenas in which to learn how to take responsibility for themselves. The internet is one such arena.

- An opportunity for creativity. There are a myriad ways in which the internet can encourage creativity, whether it is through music, art, film, photography, and many other activities. The internet is also an enabling tool for shared creativity, as individuals can work together on artistic, scientific, and other imaginative projects.

- A safe environment for young people who live in unsafe or isolated locations, or who face prejudice or harassment. This is a benefit that is not often recognised, but it is an important one. Many young people who live in inner city areas, or who live in rural areas, can turn to the internet for access to learning and other benefits that would not normally be available to them. The internet can also provide a safe space for those who experience prejudice or harassment. For such young people the internet may offer a safe forum where they know they will be free from abuse or victimisation.

Anyone who looks at what teenagers are doing today on their digital devices will see how their worlds are expanding. They will see how opportunities for exploration and the acquisition of new knowledge are afforded to all who have access to the internet. I recently watched a 13-year-old on his laptop who was looking into his family history by finding out about his great-grandfather, checking on his aunt's charity website, finding out about local history and the origin of street names, and discovering where the family car had been manufactured. Such learning activity would be unthinkable without the internet.

The threats of the internet: cyber-bullying, gaming, pornography, grooming and sexual harassment, and internet addiction

Having outlined some of the opportunities for young people that are afforded by the internet, it is time to turn to the threats. For many parents it is the threats – to privacy and to safety – that are paramount where technology is concerned. When any group of parents gets together today many of the worries and concerns centre on this topic.

In this section I will outline some of the main issues that cause anxiety for parents. Following this I will look more closely at the main ways parents can help teenagers stay safe on-line.

Cyber-bullying. In some ways this is the same as the bullying already discussed in the previous chapter, but there are important differences which make it more distressing and more difficult to deal with. First, cyber-bullying can happen at any time, day or night, and so in that sense it feels as if there is less protection. At least with physical or verbal bullying at school, the victim can get away from it, but with cyber-bullying this is much harder to do.

Another important aspect of cyber-bullying is that it often involves many different people, and of course it can be seen by anyone using the internet. This makes it especially threatening, as the person being bullied has no idea who knows about it, or how many people are involved. Lastly, cyber-bullying can be anonymous, so that the victim does not know where it is coming from. All these aspects of cyber-bullying mean that it is a particularly upsetting and troubling experience. Individuals who are the target of this type of bullying are made to feel that there is no escape, and no safe place to hide.

Cyber-bullying can also occur though sexting. This involves the sending of explicit sexual content to others on-line, and may include photos of people without clothes on, body parts such as breasts or genitalia, or people in compromising sexual situations. If sexting is used in this way it should be treated in the same way as other forms of cyber-bullying. However, its use is not restricted to bullying. As far as it is possible to tell, sexting is also being used by young people as a way of flirting or interesting a possible partner. It is illegal to send explicit sexual content to others in this way, but this does not appear to stop teenagers from using sexting for this purpose.

A typical scenario might be that a girl really wants a boy to fancy her. To attract him she sends him a photo of herself in a sexually provocative pose. She does not take into account that, once the photo is on the internet, it cannot be erased. The boy wants to boast, so he sends it on to one of his friends. Before the day has elapsed, the photo has been seen by most of the school. Young people need advice to manage the digital world, and to be able to protect themselves.

Returning to cyber-bullying, it is reasonable to ask what can be done about it? Cyber-bullying is very serious. It can cause harm to the individual, and can be a devastating experience. The problem for parents is that it may not be obvious that it is happening. The teenager may feel ashamed and helpless, and for a variety of reasons may not disclose to the parents that he or she is a victim of this type of bullying.

A teenager should not have to deal with this on their own. If any adult is aware that this type of bullying is occurring, they should help the young person find someone to talk to. The young person should keep copies of any abusive texts or messages. They should not reply to any message or email that is abusive. If necessary they can delete their profile from a social network, or create blocking devices for emails and messages. Most important of all, teenagers and parents will need good advice as to how best to deal with this situation. At the end of the book there is a list of organisations, such as Childline, which can help.

Here is one mother's experience, illustrating just how important it is to keep channels of communication open between parents and teenagers.

> The good thing about being able to talk, like in the family, you can help sometimes. It was some guy that my son knew, I forget the whole story, but anyway this guy started to text him threatening things, and he was able to tell me and his Dad, which was a good thing. We said, right, that's ok, we'll show you how to deal with this. (What did you do?) My husband and I worked out that you can block these messages so whatever he's saying … you know what I mean? We realised there was this guy at school, and he really was doing it to other people as well, and it was really threatening things that were coming through. I said: "Don't even answer those". I didn't even know how you could block messages, but we worked it out, and that was an end to that. But thank God that he'd actually said: "I've got a problem here, I'm not sure how to deal with it myself". Yes, you keep on telling them, don't you, you don't always have to deal with problems yourself, sometimes you do need to go to someone and say look, I've got a problem here.

Gaming. On-line gaming is a difficult topic to talk about as a threat, as it is so widespread among all age groups. Furthermore it is enjoyable, entertaining and lots of fun. Children as young as five or six are playing games such as Moshi Monsters and other similar on-line games. In the younger age groups both boys and girls are equally involved, but among teenagers there is no doubt that many more boys than girls are playing electronic games. If gaming is so prevalent among children and young people, what are the safety issues? There are two major concerns for parents and carers. These are:

- Electronic gaming is gripping and exciting, and therefore it can be difficult to limit the time spent on this activity,
- The content of some games is either violent or explicitly sexual, and therefore inappropriate for young people.

In terms of the time spent on this activity, parents often ask whether there is any guidance about how long an individual should be playing these games. There is no categorical guidance available on this matter, and the age of the teenager, and whether it is in the holiday or on school days, will affect the answer to this question. However, for most young people no more than one hour a day on school days would seem to be a sensible limit. On weekends and holidays two hours a day should be the maximum. If the teenager is spending more than two hours per day on gaming, this is almost certainly too much.

Some parents have reported that trying to set a limit of a certain amount of time per day is very hard, and leads to a lot of conflict. As a result families have opted for identifying one or two days per week which are games-free days, or non-technology days. This has worked well for some. Other families have contacted the parents of those teenagers who are engaged in joint gaming activities. A group of parents working together can have more sway. If a number of teenagers are all subject to the same limits, this may be a more successful strategy.

Turning now to the content of games, this also poses very difficult issues for parents. Games are classified according to a system that has been introduced by the European Union. This is known as the PEGI system, and classifies games into age bands 7+, 12+, 16+, and 18+. The system is legally enforceable for retailers, but is very difficult to observe. Many parents say they are unaware of it. Even when they are, the leakage across from other families, or from older siblings and other relatives, makes it extremely difficult to control. Here is one father's view about this.

We've done the "over 18" games, we've had that. You win some, you lose some. You can't have the blanket ban of "you're under 18, you can't play that game or watch that film", because, well, they'll just go to their friend's house, and they've got it. The whole society sets the standard, and you can't really fight against it. But we wouldn't go out and buy them an "over 18" game.

In spite of the challenges, there are many things that parents can do. Perhaps the most important thing of all is to remain involved and aware. If you give up, thinking that it is just another world which you will never understand, this is of no help to the teenager. Every young person needs to learn to set their own boundaries, but this is hard to do. They need help to set these boundaries, and this help can only come from parents. As with so many things, it may feel as if the teenager is taking no notice of you and your concerns. Without your concern and involvement, however, the teenager will have no way of learning to set boundaries themselves.

Pornography. This is another topic that is hard to discuss, as its use on-line is so widespread. Many adults access porn on the internet, and, with some exceptions, this is not illegal or even necessarily harmful. So what is the issue with teenagers? Many boys today report that the way they are learning about sex is by looking at pornography websites. This may make sense to them if they have no other means of learning about sex. Where the school is not providing what they need, and it is awkward to discuss such matters with their parents, the internet is an obvious place to turn. However, the use by boys of pornographic websites creates a problem for girls, as many find pornography intimidating. It is also hard to escape, as they may see it on someone's phone or be sent a link without searching for it themselves.

As will be obvious there are many different reasons for teenagers viewing pornography. Some may use these websites for curiosity, and give up quickly. Others may spend a lot of time looking at this material, but grow bored with it after a while. Yet others may wish to avoid it, but find this difficult because of their friends or their peer group. It is reasonable that you as a parent will feel anxious about pornography on the internet. However, if you find out that your teenager is looking at such sites, it is very important to establish the facts before you react.

You do not need to get into a panic about pornography. If your teenager has accessed a site which shows pornographic images, do find out what is happening. How often has this occurred? Are other children or young people involved? Can the teenager talk about this in a sensible way, or is this a hidden and shameful issue? Most important, consider whether there are opportunities for the young person to find out about sex in more healthy ways. Leaving a good book on sex in an obvious place in the house can work well. It may also be possible to have a reasonable discussion with your teenager. Talking about sex with your teenager is a topic that is included at the end of Chapter 10.

The major risks associated with accessing pornography on the internet are twofold. In the first place it is possible that this behaviour will become addictive. If someone is repeatedly exposed to images that are over-stimulating, and if they have limited resources to restrict this exposure, then this can become a serious problem. In such cases the young person will need some help to deal with this behaviour.

The second risk has to do with the impact of pornography on sexual behaviour. Pornographic images are demeaning to women, and may well be confusing to young people if these images imply that violent or abusive sex is normal. Do teenagers who are exposed to pornography develop a distorted or disturbed view of sex? This is a legitimate concern, but it will very much depend on the attitudes to sex within the family, and the opportunities the young person has to learn about sex in a healthy manner. It seems unlikely that a young person's sexual development will be influenced by pornography unless: (1) they become addicted to pornographic images; or (2) there are other behavioural problems to compound the impact of pornography.

The surest way to protect a teenager from the risks of pornography is to be aware of what is happening to them, and to make it safe for them to talk to you about sex. The fact that your teenager has looked at pornographic images on-line is not a catastrophe. Only a tiny minority of young people suffer from addiction to pornography. The relationship you have with your teenager is the most protective factor. The more support you can give, and the more these matters can be discussed openly, the less likely it will be that any harm will be caused by pornography on the internet.

Grooming and sexual harassment. Large numbers of teenagers use chat rooms and social networking sites. This is an enjoyable and appealing activity, partly because it is a way of making new friends, and partly because it can be a way of re-inventing yourself by trying out different images and identities. For young people both these objectives can be of great importance.

If a teenager is without friends or is struggling with friendships in the real world, then finding friends on-line is an obvious thing to do. It should be remembered that the on-line dating industry for adults is booming, and growing all the time. It is not just teenagers who turn to the internet to improve their social life! As far as identity development is concerned, again the internet provides the ideal arena for this to take place. Where better to work out who you are than a space where there is so much freedom and anonymity?

Having said this, the risk of grooming is one that cannot be ignored. Grooming is the term used to describe the behaviour of a predator who targets young people on-line to get them to meet off-line for the purpose of sex. There are many strategies used by such people, including offers of gifts, money, sympathy, or even modelling jobs. The goal of the predator is to get the young person to feel "special", and therefore comfortable enough so that they will be willing to meet in person.

Grooming is illegal in the UK, and on-line predators can be prosecuted. Those most at risk of such predatory activity are young people who are vulnerable, those who lack support and love at home, and those who need "validation" from a source outside the family. I will be discussing how to stay safe on-line in another section, but for the moment it is worth emphasising the role of parents here. Make sure this subject is discussed. Keep the dialogue going on topics to do with internet safety. Make it clear to your teenager that you want to be sure they are safe when using chat rooms and other sites. Above all try to provide the support they need. Even if they are pushing you away, keep sending the message that you care, and that you are there for them if they ever need help.

Internet addiction. Only a tiny minority of young people can be said to have internet addiction. However, this is another worry for parents. The question of how to limit the time teenagers spend on the internet is something that baffles many people. Here is one mother's experience with her son.

> He'd left school, couldn't get a job, he was going on to some training scheme, and I said to him, you know, you can't carry on playing this blinking game, because at the time he was playing World of Warcraft. I didn't realise actually, looking back now, that's why he was completely … it was just really bad. And now he tells me he was completely head first into that game and we didn't know it. It basically took his life away, because he was just playing this game,

constantly, constantly. I didn't even know that he was even staying up at night and playing this game, his bedroom was downstairs, and he was away from our bedroom. I've always let my kids have their own time and their own space, so unbeknown to me this game had completely taken over his life.

As will be apparent from the previous sections, a number of on-line activities can become addictive. Gaming and pornography are two obvious examples, but even the use of chat rooms and social networking sites can consume enormous amounts of time. It is for this reason that the involvement of parents becomes so important. Young people will need help to set the boundaries. Most will not be able to do this entirely on their own. I want to turn now to looking in more detail at what parents can do.

What can parents do?

As I have been saying throughout this chapter, if at all possible it will help if parents can stay involved, as they have an important role to play. However, to many this seems like an impossible mountain to climb. There are three things that make this particularly hard for parents.

- A skills gap. To begin with, it will appear to many that young people understand the digital world, while adults do not. Young people navigate their way around, seeming to know exactly what to do, while parents look on in awe.
- A foreign country. In addition to the differences in skills, there is also the fact that some things on the internet simply appear to be in a foreign language. It is hard for an onlooker to grasp what is involved in some of the on-line games. To many parents it can appear as if it is another world which is difficult to access.
- Pushing the parent away. The third point is that, in some situations, young people resist the involvement of parents. Some teenagers go through a stage when they want to keep their parents as far away as possible. In such circumstances it can be very hard indeed for parents to find a common language and a means of keeping the dialogue going.

The barriers that I have mentioned may seem too daunting to be tackled. However, these problems have to be overcome if young people are to get the support they need. If teenagers are to stay safe on-line, they will need some input from their parents. How can this be achieved? I will outline three elements of a positive approach that parents can take in response to the challenges of the digital world. These are:

- media monitoring,
- tailoring your response to the age of the young person,
- keeping your son or daughter safe on-line.

Media monitoring. This is a term used to describe the behaviour of parents when they oversee the use of the internet by their sons and daughters. The way parents respond will depend on their level of anxiety, and on their general parenting style. If a parent leans towards an authoritarian style, they will want to set the rules and remain in control. If they lean towards an indulgent style they may believe that they can leave the young person to work it out for themselves.

A third style, the style I talked about in Chapter 6, is the authoritative style. Parents who lean towards this approach will be inclined to work with the young person to agree the most sensible and acceptable approach. Parents using the authoritative style will not shy away from talking about privacy and safety, but will not try and impose their own solutions. They will recognise the teenager's need to become independent, but will make clear their own concerns. They will be most likely to seek a negotiated approach, where parent and young person together think through what is best.

There is no doubt that the digital world throws up special challenges for parents. However, the parent's response should, if at all possible, be much the same as their response to any other threat or problem faced by the young person.

In discussions on media monitoring a distinction has been made between two approaches:

- active mediation
- restrictive mediation.

This distinction is similar to the parenting styles I have just been outlining. In essence active mediation involves engaging with the young person, and working it out together. An example would be: "The parent helps the teenager learn how to stop any experience on-line that makes the teenager feel uncomfortable". As far as restrictive mediation is concerned, as the reader can imagine, this involves more control on the part of the parent. An example would be: "The parent holds a secure password, preventing the teenager from downloading any material from the internet unless it has been vetted by the parent".

The evidence shows that young people respond best to active mediation. This allows them to be involved in decisions, and makes it clear that the parent is not taking control away from them. However, the approach of the parent should be appropriate to the age of the young person, and this is the topic I will turn to next.

The age and capacity of the young person. Parents will want to tailor the type of mediation and monitoring to the age and capacity of the young person. The age range of those involved in on-line activity is very wide, with children as young as five or six playing on-line games and sending messages. Clearly there has to be a graded response, with more control being exercised for the younger age groups. Simply put, there should be a higher degree of restrictive mediation for the 6-10-year age group, with a gradual introduction of active mediation as the individual enters the teenage years.

Having said this, there can be no hard and fast rules about what parents should do at different ages. Each child is different, and the best response will be tailored to the needs of the individual. For example, one 10-year-old girl will be mature for her age, and will expect to have a say in how to manage her on-line activities. Another girl at this age will need a more structured approach, with tighter boundaries and more advice and guidance about how to stay safe. Parents should aim to balance the degree of active and restrictive mediation according to both the age of the individual and to their particular personality and capabilities.

While it is true that the age of the young person will influence a parent's response, guidance from an adult will still be essential during the teenage years. Even those in the 11–14-year age range will need guidance on the risks posed by the internet. As one example, teenagers do not always take on board that once a message or image has been sent on-line, it cannot be retrieved. Once something is sent on-line, it is there for good. A young person may know this intellectually, but it is easy to forget.

A useful exercise sometimes used by teachers is as follows. You ask a young person to take a piece of paper and screw it up into a ball. Then the task is to flatten the paper out so that the folds and creases disappear. Of course this cannot be done. The exercise is a concrete example of how it is impossible to get rid of images once they are on the internet. It can be tried at home too!

Keeping your son or daughter safe on-line. There is no simple answer to this. There is no magic wand to be waved which will automatically protect the young person from all the threats in the digital world. However, that is true of life in general. We cannot protect our teenagers all the time and in every circumstance. They have to go out there and learn about the world, and develop skills to cope with the possibility of harm. The digital world is exactly the same. The role of the parent is not to provide the cotton wool so that the teenager is shielded from harm. The role of the parent is to help the young person develop the skills to cope with threats and danger.

There are four main ways in which you, as a parent, can help a young person stay safe on-line. These are:

- Encouraging your teenager to remember the maxim "Think before you post". The central point here is that nothing is private in the on-line world. As someone once said, if you wouldn't print it on a T-shirt and walk down the street with it on, don't post it on-line. While young people might have the sense that they are only talking to a close friend, or to a few friends, this is not the case. Whatever they say, whatever message they send, whatever picture they upload, can be seen by anyone with access to the internet. Parents should have an ongoing discussion with the young person about privacy and how people can protect themselves by being careful about what gets on to the internet.

- Understanding the technology and how it can protect your teenager. Earlier I quoted a mother whose son was receiving threatening messages. She did not know that her son could use a blocking mechanism, but she and her husband worked it out. There are many ways in which technology can help here, whether it is a pop-up message about unsafe material, a family friendly filter, a blocking process, or other mechanisms to alert the user about something that is unsafe. Parents and teenagers together can inform themselves about how technology works to protect the user.

- Making sure there are some boundaries in terms of time spent on-line. I have already talked about this in relation to gaming. General guidance on gaming suggests no more than one hour a day on school days, and perhaps double that on weekends and holidays. It is also suggested that, for health reasons, an individual should take a break from the screen every half hour. However, there is a wider issue. With the advent of smart phones, and the use of the digital space for homework and other activities, it is hard to restrict screen time. Many experts are now arguing that it is more to do with what the young person is doing on-line, rather than with how much time is spent on-line. However, we have to acknowledge that on-screen activities can be compelling, and it may be hard for young people to set the boundaries themselves. This is where parents come in. If parents can create a safe structure in the home, with clear limits for activities such as gaming, this will help teenagers to learn in time to do this for themselves.

- Being engaged with your teenager's on-line activity. There is no point in denying that this brings all sorts of challenges. It is hard for parents to remain engaged with the teenager's on-line activity. However, I do not mean that the parent has to sit next to the young person, looking over their shoulder every five minutes. What is necessary, though, is that the parent remains engaged. This means being aware of how much time is being spent on-line, and in broad terms understanding the scope of the teenager's on-line activities. This will enable the parent to keep talking about this issue, to be firm where appropriate, and to demonstrate care and concern.

13

DIVORCE AND THE
CHANGING FAMILY

My Mum and Dad have split up, so my Mum lives at the top
of the town and my Dad lives down here, so I can always go
to one of them if I need. Like I've done in the past, have an
argument with my Mum and come to stay at my Dad's. I've
got all my friends around the place too and some of them –
their parents are the same as well, so sometimes I go and stay
at a friend's house, or they come and stay at mine, and we
can just talk about it.

(15-year-old girl)

In this girl's world it appears unremarkable that parents split up,
teenagers move from one parent to another, and there will be friends
who are also affected by divorce. Families are changing, and many
readers will recognise this picture. Divorce, separation, new partners,
and reconstituted families are a part of many people's lives today.
Yet while this picture may be familiar, there remain many difficulties
and challenges for both parents and young people. In this chapter, I
will address some of these difficulties, while also reflecting on the
positives of new and reconstituted families.

As with many other topics in the book, it will be hard to cover all
the ground concerning such a wide range of issues, and at the end of
the book there will be pointers to other books, websites, and organisations which provide further information on changing families. Here
I will consider the following subjects:

- divorce and its impact on parents and teenagers,
- limiting the harm of family breakdown,
- step-parents and new partners,
- lone parents.

I will first reflect briefly on the STAGE framework and its implications for divorce and the changing family.

The STAGE framework

The STAGE framework has relevance to many of the issues I will consider in this chapter. The significance of parents, the importance of good two-way communication, and the appropriate exercise of authority are all absolutely central to maintaining strong positive relationships with teenagers during or after a divorce. While all these are important, I want to emphasise here the E for Emotion. When considering the outcome of family breakdown it is clear that there will be a massive emotional impact on any child or teenager affected by such a major process. Therefore the E needs to be given careful consideration.

I have noted that during the teenage years, as a result of the changes in the brain, there will be times when managing emotion will be hard in any event. However, when something as profound as parental divorce occurs, this difficulty in emotion regulation will be magnified. It is essential therefore for parents to take into account the emotions that are created by a major change in family organisation. Adults need to recognise the painful and confusing feelings that are likely to be created in the young people involved. It is understandable that parents may want to avoid acknowledging the feelings of the teenagers. This just increases the pain. However, avoiding the emotions will simply lead to further problems at a later stage. Any adult experiencing family breakdown should give careful consideration to the E for Emotion when thinking about the needs of teenagers in these circumstances.

Divorce and its impact on parents and teenagers

Divorce is a major life change for all who are affected by it. It usually brings with it alterations in all aspects of family life, including housing, financial arrangements, support for each family member, the division of household tasks, and many other matters. For most people divorce is almost certainly going to be a painful and distressing experience, although there may be benefits too. One key thing to remember is that divorce is not a single event, but part of a long process. To understand divorce and its impact it is necessary to consider what came before, and what happens after the two parents separate.

In situations where there was serious conflict between the parents before the divorce, then children may feel some relief once separation has taken place. On the other hand if disputes and arguments between parents continue after divorce, children and young people will find adjustment much harder.

As a further example of the fact that divorce is not a single event but a process, some young people may be upset or distressed at first, but once the initial shock is over they may adjust well. Others may seem fine in the early stages, but gradually become more affected, possibly because of the changed relationship with the parent who has left home.

One of the questions frequently asked by parents is whether the age of the child or young person makes a difference to their subsequent adjustment to divorce. Here are two views.

> I think a major factor is that we were divorced when they were older, rather than younger. If we had been divorced when they were 7 or 8 I think children adapt much better. But my son was 16 and I realise now it affected him more than the younger one.

> One of the biggest problems must be that me and her father were divorced at a very critical time, when she was growing up at an emotional time. She was 10, and she could not come to terms with the fact that we split up then.

As will be apparent, people are very much influenced by their individual experiences. Age does make a difference, in that the older the young person, the more likely they are to be able to make sense of what has happened. However, teenagers can be just as affected as younger children, although they may show their distress in different ways. Young children can become clingy and demanding, or show their anger through temper tantrums. Teenagers, on the other hand, may become withdrawn or show their resentment by acting out and getting involved in risky behaviour.

However important age is, other factors remain extremely important in determining the individual's reaction to divorce. The continuing relationship with the parent who leaves home, and the degree of ongoing conflict between the parents may have just as much of an impact as the age of the young person.

This leads on to the question of whether it is possible for children and young people to adjust successfully to divorce. The straightforward answer to this is yes – it is possible to adjust to divorce. However, there are many factors involved. Much will depend on the circumstances of the family, and on the continuing relationships with both parents following separation. Here is one father's experience.

> Well yes, it works well, but then we're lucky. We're lucky I think because we've been mature about it. There was no third party involved when we got divorced, and we never even saw a solicitor, we did everything on-line, we got the forms, we filled them in and signed them, paid the £180 or whatever it was for the court fees, and that's it! ... We do things slightly differently, but I try to do the same things as her, like on homework. She's probably stricter than me. We've got our differences, which is not surprising since we're divorced! But we talk about it, or I get talked to! But now we're divorced I probably say more of what I think than what I did before, and what I should have done before when we were together.

All the evidence is clear in showing that the most important factors influencing the adjustment of young people following divorce are:

- the continuing relationship between the mother and father,
- the relationship the teenager maintains with both parents.

There are, of course, other factors which will make a difference. Having to move house and change school is likely to be difficult. Making a new relationship with a step-parent or live-in partner may lead to conflict and stress. Many families experience financial hardship after divorce, and this too can have a powerful impact on a teenager who may resent the fact that there is less money around.

Nonetheless it is the relationship with the two biological parents that is the most critical factor. Teenagers need both parents. Of course a young person will find ways of compensating for the loss of a father or mother. However, to carry a sense of having been rejected by a parent is very hard indeed. Where relationships can be maintained with both parents this represents the best chance for good adjustment following divorce. Where young people experience rejection there will be a lot of pain and distress.

Here is a mother talking about her daughter, and the impact of rejection by the father.

She could not come to terms with the fact that her father did not want to know her. She would not come to terms with it. She tried to make excuses for her father's lack of interest. He didn't even want to see her and her sister. I think she was greatly hurt and couldn't understand why he didn't want to see her. Emotionally it must have been a great strain on her to realise that her father did not love her any more. She did not accept that, and I think she's fought that. I think that is where her aggression has come out, and who can blame her?

Limiting the harm of family breakdown

There are a number of different ways in which the possible harm that flows from a family breakdown can be reduced or mitigated. Here I will consider some of the steps that parents can take to help young people adjust to the change in family circumstances.

The first point to make is that preparation, although difficult, will make a big difference to any child or young person. As one teenager put it:

It was as if we didn't exist. Something was going on, but nobody told us. How could they forget it was our lives they were messing around with?

This is a really important point. It is often the case that adults are so caught up in their own distress that they lose sight of the needs of the children in the family. Children and young people need to be prepared, if at all possible, for what is going to happen. The more young people are left in the dark, the more fears and anxieties are left to fester. This is how one mother put it:

You must try to let the children know that it is nothing to do with them, because it is quite often felt that way. And they feel they should have been able to stop it or that it was something that they did. And it's amazing how many times I've spoken to people and that's how they feel.

It is easy for parents to feel that the children won't understand, or that whatever they say will be too disturbing. In fact it is more upsetting to be left in the dark. The more opportunity there is for children and young people to be prepared for the changes that are going to happen, the better it will be.

The next point to make has to do with continuing conflict between parents. As I have already pointed out, what happens after the divorce or separation is critical for adjustment. The worst possible situation is one in which the young person feels as if they are "caught in the middle" of an ongoing conflict.

> I think it was the hate between the two of them. Knowing how much they hated each other and being in the middle of that. That was really awful. They were so horrible to each other all the time, and all they'd do was slag each other off to me. And I hated it, I really hated it. I felt really in the middle, and like I couldn't do anything. I think at first I felt like part of it was my fault and I should have stopped it but, I mean, I just couldn't. But I always carry it around, that I should have been able to stop it.
>
> (18-year-old young woman)

Over the last two decades many research studies have pointed out the damage that continuing conflict can cause. As a result it is now generally recognised that it is important to avoid ongoing disputes if at all possible. There are more opportunities today than there were in the past for mediation for parents before divorce. This is a good thing. Every support should be given to couples so that continuing conflict, particularly conflict that involves the children, can be avoided at all costs.

So far I have noted two key strategies for limiting harm following divorce:

- finding ways of preparing children and young people for the change that is about to happen,
- ensuring that they do not have the experience of being caught in the middle of an ongoing conflict.

A third strategy has to do with being open, acknowledging the painful feelings that are bound to arise as a result of family break-up. One mother put it like this:

> If the break-up is taking place with teenage children, be very honest with them. Talk about it, talk about it as much as they want.

This is not always easy. It takes courage, but it will make a huge difference in the end. All members of the family will experience upsetting feelings. Everyone at some time will experience sadness, loss, anger, and anxiety about the future. The only way to deal with this is to be open with the young people involved, allowing them to express their feelings. This will be painful for the adults, but it is the best way for the feelings to be managed. If expression of emotions is not allowed, then the distress may well be demonstrated through challenging or difficult behaviour.

In some families talking about these things can be extremely difficult. Some parents may feel they simply cannot handle the young person's resentment and sense of loss. Other parents may be in such a state themselves that they cannot talk about the situation without losing control of their own emotions. In such circumstances parents may need outside help.

There is no shame in looking outside the family for this support. It is not good if these things are swept under the carpet. It is far better for young people if they can be given the opportunity to acknowledge and explore their feelings. Divorce is painful. The more children and young people can be supported through this process, the easier it will be for parents in the long run.

Step-parents and new partners

Some years ago it would have been sufficient in this section to talk only about step-parents. Today there are many different family arrangements, and it is for this reason that I include here new partners. These may be adults who are live-in partners or those living elsewhere yet still playing a role as a partner to the biological parent. This section applies to those adults who, in whatever form, have a relationship with a teenager without being a biological parent.

I should say a word about age. In the previous section I argued that, while age matters in some respects in influencing the impact of divorce, other factors play a very large part too. Where step-parents and new partners are concerned, age is almost certainly a key element in determining the role of a new adult appearing in the family. The younger the child, the more likely it is that a new partner can play a role as a substitute parent. For teenagers, however, this may not be appropriate.

I will have more to say about what role a new partner can expect to fulfil later in this section. For the moment it is important to note that the age of the young person is critical here. Teenagers are likely to be extremely sensitive about "divided loyalties". They will not want to see a new partner stepping into the shoes of a parent who is no longer living in the family home.

136

The arrival of a new partner in the family will generate strong emotions. Unless these are recognised and attended to, everyone will be in for a bumpy ride. It may sound obvious, but some degree of resentment and jealousy will be inevitable. A new partner will be capturing the time and attention, not to mention the love, of the parent. Any young person will struggle to come to terms with this situation. The more the parent and the new partner can acknowledge this, and allow for a period of adjustment, the more likely things are to settle down.

It is also important to stress that giving the young person a chance to prepare for the arrival of a new partner can make a difference. Taking things slowly and finding ways for the teenager to get to know the new partner will pay dividends in the long run. This is not to say it will all run smoothly. Nevertheless it is important to make opportunities for the young person to get to know the new partner gradually. This can provide space for some of the feelings to be explored before a major change in the family occurs.

I have already referred to the question of divided loyalties. This is something that is really important to children and young people. It is not difficult to see that making a relationship with a new adult can feel like a "betrayal" of loyalty to the parent who is no longer living at home. This concern is also often reflected in the problem of how to handle differences between two homes. If the teenager is spending time with both parents, then there may well be a tension between the two sets of standards and values. Young people will need help to handle these tensions. The more parents can do to communicate, and to provide shared parenting, the better off the young person will be.

The next topic to consider here is sexuality. Sexuality is an important issue in all families, but in step-families or with new partners it can be especially troublesome. All teenagers have great difficulty accepting their parents' sexuality. However, with new partnerships young people are brought face-to-face with a sexually active parent. Because of jealousy and other emotions sexuality can become a symbol for everything that is intolerable about the new family arrangements.

If the teenager is behaving oddly, it is worth considering whether sex has anything to do with it. Some young people may wish to change bedrooms so as not to hear what is going on at night. Others may leave the room abruptly if there is any physical contact between the parent and new partner. However extreme these reactions may appear, for some teenagers the parent's new sexual relationship may seem literally unbearable.

Parents, step-parents, and new partners should think carefully about their behaviour in this regard. It is important not to be sexually provocative. This includes keeping the bedroom and bathroom doors closed and avoiding been seen in an undressed state. It is also important for adults to be discrete about expressions of affection such as kissing and cuddling. Privacy should be maintained, and parents and new partners should be sensitive to the teenager's feelings where sexuality is concerned.

It is now time to consider the role of the step-parent or new partner with a teenager. Many people who have been in this position will say it is hard to get it right. Most adults in this role will have experienced rejection, insults, or difficult behaviour from their new step-son or daughter. One step-father told me about his step-daughter who ran away from home in the middle of the night because she could not stand the thought of her mother being in a bed together with a man she hated.

The starting point is that the step-parent is not a substitute parent. This means that the boundaries are different. A step-parent cannot presume that what would be acceptable for their own son or daughter will be acceptable for a teenager in a new relationship. This is true of all aspects of life from putting an arm round the shoulder to criticising table manners. In most cases a new partner or step-parent cannot have the same intimacy, cannot share the same confidences, and needs to accept that this is the case.

It is probably the issue of control that causes the biggest headaches for step-parents and new partners. From the teenager's point of view the new partner does not have the same rights as the biological parent. From the step-parents point of view, however, there may be times when some control has to be exercised, especially if the parent is not at home. This issue can only be resolved by discussion, and by negotiation between all members of the family. The right to exercise control can be conferred on a new partner or step-parent, but this needs to be agreed openly, and acknowledged by the teenager. Unless this is done disagreement and resentment are inevitable.

Here is an example of a mother describing just such a situation with her son and her new partner, the boy's step-father:

> It's almost like two testosterone beings, they are suddenly ...
> my husband sees him as a threat. Until a year ago my son
> was just pootling along, just going to school, keeping his
> head down, and then all of a sudden he's got more of a
> voice, and he's obviously got on my side now much more,

and my husband gauges that. My son is quite good, he just bows down and walks away from it, and then when (stepfather) is out of the house he will have a go at me and say "What did you let him do that for?". 'Cause obviously your own father you're going to accept different, aren't you? So that's made it difficult because I feel like I'm piggy in the middle. It's so difficult for me having to be on one side, and then on the other all the time. It's quite stressful because either I agree with my son, but on the other hand you know, obviously I agree with my husband so it's difficult, I'm in the middle.

This is a tough position to be in. We can all recognise how uncomfortable it will be to feel that one is in the middle of an ongoing situation of this sort. As I have said, the only viable option in such circumstances will be:

- recognition of the problem by all who are affected,
- open discussion with everyone concerned.
- negotiation over how to resolve it.

Turning now to the role of a step-parent, where there is conflict such as that described above there is little chance for the adult to play a constructive role with the young person. However, in the best of circumstances the role of step-parent can be described as that of a good friend. This is someone who can be a companion, who can share interests or leisure activities, who can be a useful source of ideas and opinions, and who can provide support at the appropriate times. Most important of all, the role of a step-parent is to take things slowly, to stand back, and to wait until the young person comes to them.

Of course it is not easy for a teenager and a step-parent to become good friends. This takes a long time, and requires a lot of patience. Friendship has to be earned, through respect and understanding. There are few guidelines which define the role of a step-parent or new partner. It is something that each individual creates by his or her own efforts. The most successful step-parents are those who start with no expectations at all. These adults are the ones who are able to put their needs second, and let time take its course.

Lone parents

Being a lone parent following divorce or separation can be very hard. In the early stages things may look extremely bleak. Some people are overcome with guilt, worrying about what they have done to cause the break-up of the marriage. Others may feel completely rejected and lost, unsure if they can keep going as a parent in this situation. The early years following divorce are difficult to live through, and it may be sensible for someone in this situation to seek extra support to come to terms with what has happened.

Things will change, and as time passes most people manage to readjust. The children in the family will need help to settle into the new arrangements. If at all possible a system should be established by which they can have contact with the parent who has left home. For younger children regular visits or contact are important, but as teenagers get older they will want to have more control over access arrangements. This may mean that patterns of contact are not so regular, but the key thing is that these are maintained and facilitated by both parents.

Lone parents have particular challenges to face. One of these has to do with fulfilling both roles at once. In a two-parent family it is possible for one adult to keep hold of the boundaries and set the limits, while the other can offer a shoulder to cry on. When one parent has to carry out both these roles it can be confusing and stressful for everyone in the family. This is especially true when the parent is going through a period of adjustment to the new circumstances, as this mother describes.

> In the first year I was far too soft and fuzzy about my boundaries. I was really going through a hard emotional time, and they were pushing me and testing me and seeing how far they could go. You sort of feel guilty. I think it's when you don't know where you are, and you feel guilty because you're separated. Once I'd firmed them up, and I knew where I stood, then the children knew where I stood and they weren't out of control any more.

In this case the mother saw what was needed, and as she recovered her own resilience she was able to set the boundaries that the young people needed. However, this is not always the case. Many parents who are on their own feel lonely, and turn to their sons and daughters – especially daughters – for support. This is something that has to be watched carefully.

On the one hand teenagers will of course respond to the needs of a parent, and will enjoy the closeness that results. On the other teenagers do need their parents to be parents: to set boundaries but also to allow increasing autonomy. Too much intimacy between parent and teenager can be confusing, and will not necessarily help the young person to develop in a healthy manner.

Following divorce many lone parents have to deal with the teenager's anger. This can be over-the-top, irrational anger, rather like the temper tantrums of younger children. This anger can fly about all over the place, often being expressed at inappropriate moments and in inappropriate places. It will help to remember that the teenager may have a lot to be angry about. There will be feelings of rejection and loss. There may well be fury at the fact that "normal" family life has disappeared, to be replaced by new relationships and uncertain circumstances.

It will be hard to deal with this anger, but it has to be recognised, acknowledged, and talked about. Trying to avoid it or ignore it will not help. The teenager will need support to come to terms with what has happened to the family. Often that support can come from the parents. If they can be open, and allow the young person to express these feelings, this will mean that over time the emotion may become easier to manage. One father, faced with an angry son, responded like this:

> I tried to increase my verbal feelings about him. I told him that I loved him, and cared about him, and that he was special. I said that he could always talk to me. I really looked at everything I hadn't said to him, and tried to be as frank and open as I could about my feelings for him.

Finally, lone parents should hold on to the fact that they have needs too. Many single parents wear themselves out trying to be a super-parent making up for all the things that have been lost. In doing so they forget that they are human beings themselves. Lone parents need support and they need time for themselves. The more lone parents can find this support for themselves the easier it will be to meet the needs of the young people in the family.

Conclusion

I will conclude with a note about the positives that can stem from divorce or from being in a reconstituted family. In the beginning of the chapter I said I would reflect on these positives. I mentioned that where a child or young person has had to live in the middle of serious battles between parents, there may be relief that this is no longer happening. We should not underestimate the effect that ongoing conflict of this sort has on young people. Growing up in a family where this occurs can feel like a huge burden. While there will of course be complicated feelings created as a result of divorce, once the young person no longer has to live in the middle of ongoing conflict, there will undoubtedly be a sense of a burden being lifted.

Two other positives should be mentioned. First, with new and reconstituted families, it may be that a teenager will be able to take on new roles. These roles may allow for increased autonomy and responsibility. Where there are two parents in the family young people can be held back from taking on adult roles, even though they may be ready for increased responsibility. Following divorce or in a new family there may be scope for a teenager to take on a more mature role which provides an opportunity for growth and development.

Second, it is important to recognise that new relationships with step-parents or with live-in partners can offer much that is positive. Much of the discussion about step-parents tends to focus on the challenges and difficulties, and I have rehearsed some of these in this chapter. However, there are many opportunities for good things to come out of a new relationship with an adult who is not a biological parent. In the best of circumstances adults in this role can offer support, companionship, and a very special type of friendship unlike that to be gained from any other adult.

14

RISK-TAKING AND CHALLENGING BEHAVIOUR

In this chapter I will deal with some of the topics that are most troubling for parents. Throughout this book I have mentioned a number of issues, such as bullying, depression, unsuitable friends, and so on that that are of concern. Here, however, I will tackle some of the most difficult areas. I will not be able to deal with all the worries that parents have. This book was never intended to be a textbook about troubled teenagers. Nonetheless I will cover some of the ground that relates to risk-taking and challenging behaviour.

In the first section of the chapter I want to consider the question of risk-taking. Many parents I talk to have questions about this.

- Why do teenagers have a poor understanding of risk?
- Are some teenagers more likely to take risks than others?
- What can parents do to help teenagers avoid risky behaviour?

I will cover four areas here. These are: what is involved in risky behaviour; why teenagers might take more risks than other age groups; the difference between risky behaviour and experimentation; and finally, some consideration of factors that may protect the young person from engaging in risky behaviour.

The STAGE framework

I want to say a brief word about the STAGE framework before going on to discuss these questions. As in previous chapters it seems likely that all aspects of the framework can apply in equal measure to the topic of risk. As I will point out in a minute one key to this is the S for Significance. If we are thinking about how to protect young people from serious or harmful risk-taking, then there is no doubt that the role of the parents is central here. T for Two-way communication also has a part to play. The less young people feel able to talk to the important adults around them, the more likely they are to be pulled into the sphere of influence of unsuitable friends. Being able to keep open the channels of communication is particularly important as a protective factor. Then we can also point to the A for Authority. The way authority is exercised affects the degree of influence the parent can expect to have in the life of their teenager. As you can see, there are a myriad of ways that the STAGE framework helps us to understand all aspects of teenage behaviour. Nowhere is this more true than in the case of risky behaviour.

Risky behaviour

This is a term which is used quite loosely to cover many types of behaviour. Risky behaviour can involve the young person engaging in casual sex, drinking too much, or taking drugs. In extreme cases the term risky behaviour might be used to describe something like walking along a railway line at night. Clearly, these behaviours differ in the risk they pose.

Risky behaviour is that which has the potential to harm the individual. However, there is a continuum from very serious harm on the one hand to mild or limited harm on the other. Smoking a cannabis joint at a party is very different from driving a stolen car or sleeping rough on the streets. It is important to be clear about what is being referred to as risky behaviour.

It is also important to understand the context of the behaviour. Some behaviours such as heavy drinking might be more risky if done alone than in a group. Other behaviours such as being very out late at night may be more risky in a dangerous part of town than in a more familiar area where neighbours would be aware of what was happening.

One of the worrying things about applying the term risky behaviour to teenagers is that it can lead to everyone in this age group being classed as a problem. If adults think all teenagers are reckless or irresponsible, then this is damaging to young people and to society generally. It is important to recognise that not all teenagers take risks, and that some types of risk-taking are potentially more harmful than others.

Why teenagers might take risks

There are good reasons why some (but not all) teenagers may engage in risk-taking behaviour. One of these reasons has to do with the adolescent brain. As I mentioned in Chapter 2, recent research has given us an important insight into brain development at this age. While the brain develops rapidly during the teenage years, we have learnt that not all areas of the brain develop at the same rate. In particular the area associated with thinking and reasoning matures at a slower pace than the area associated with emotion, arousal, reward, and interest in new experiences.

This has led researchers to conclude that, for a time, young people may have more of a tendency to take risks. During this time teenagers will be less likely to think forward, to plan, and to consider the future consequences of their actions. Young people may appear to "live in the moment". They may feel invincible, or they may believe that negative consequences of risky behaviour are not going to happen to them. This is one reason why some teenagers have a poor understanding of risk.

Here is one father's view.

> Remember they are learning still. They haven't got old heads on young shoulders. They cannot realise there is a tomorrow. I do think young people think that today is the only day, whereas as parents we can see that life does go on a bit longer. I think as well when you are in your mid-teens you do feel you know it all, and it is not until you get a lot older that you suddenly realise that you do not know anything at all!

I should stress that there are very big individual differences. Not all teenagers take risks. Even those who do take risks may not necessarily expose themselves to any major harm. Nicola Morgan has written a book about teenagers called *Blame my brain*. However, we have to be very careful with this type of thinking. Many factors come into play in affecting risky behaviour in teenagers. The brain is only one of these factors. As not all teenagers take risks, we have to look at why teenagers differ, and at what other factors are influential here.

It is important to mention two other things which are linked to risky behaviour. These are peer group pressure, and low self-esteem. The first point to make is that the peer group can be very influential, and those with low self-esteem are more likely to be influenced by the peer group than those with higher self-worth. The second point to make is that those with low self-esteem may be attracted to peer groups that are more likely to engage in risk-taking.

Why should this be so? If a young person feels especially low in self-worth, they will be looking for ways to find friends and to be included. Engaging in risky behaviour may seem like a route to being noticed and being liked. Those with low self-esteem can easily gravitate to peer groups that are less sensible or responsible. They are the ones who will themselves engage in risk-taking, and will encourage others to do so too.

As I have been emphasising, there are many factors which play their part in influencing risk-taking among teenagers. Often these factors will work together. A combination of a particular stage of brain development, low self-esteem, and peer group pressure can all contribute to engagement in risky behaviour. Before I come on to look at the factors that protect young people from risk I want to consider the difference between experimentation and risk-taking.

Experimentation and risk-taking

Many commentators have pointed out that some risk-taking during the teenage years can be a positive thing. The argument goes as follows. The teenage years are a time when individuals have to learn to be safe and to protect themselves from harm. Just as a toddler has to learn that fire is dangerous, so teenagers have to learn how to protect themselves against harm where drugs and alcohol are concerned. How can they do this? They certainly won't learn just by being told that drinking too much is dangerous. They have to learn through their own experiences.

It is for this reason that it is important to draw a distinction between risk-taking and experimentation. Behaviour that involves learning, and does not pose too great a risk to safety or to health could be said to be experimentation. A teenager might think to themselves: "How much alcohol can I drink and still be safe?". Or "What is it like to smoke a joint, and how will I feel afterwards?". These are reasonable questions. Every teenager will have too much to drink at some time, and most will learn by the experience. Engaging in such behaviour is clearly part of growing up, and is a necessary part of the learning process.

This is different from a situation where young people engage in dangerous behaviour that has the potential to be seriously harmful. In this sense regular drug use, binge drinking, unsafe sex with strangers, and other similar behaviours can be seen to be very different from experimentation. It is important for you as a parent to be able to draw this distinction. Taking mild risks that involve learning is not the same as serious and continuous risk-taking. If you can recognise this, and tailor your response accordingly, this will make relationships with your teenager a lot easier to manage.

Here is one mother's story of her daughter having too much to drink.

> She did get terribly drunk one night, that was just stupidity. She was staying round her friend's house, and the parents were out. They started on Southern Comfort, they knocked it back too quick and thought this is alright, nothing has happened, so then they went on to something else, and something else again. The Dad actually phoned me at 2 in the morning and he was so apologetic. It was just one of those things. I was like do they need to go to hospital, and he was like no, and I was there in the morning and I yelled at her, and we both cried, and she was ill for a couple of days. I explained: "You could actually have died there", and I think in a way it was a good thing because she did go over the top and I think it probably did scare her. She was really ill for a couple of days, and I think from then, she'll have a drink but I don't think she'll get legless like that again.

Factors that protect from risk

From all that has been said about the role of parents, it will not come as any surprise to learn that one of the major protective factors against serious risk-taking is the family. There are many research studies that show lower levels of risk-taking among teenagers who have supportive parents. To put it another way, those who become involved in serious risk-taking behaviours may well be those whose families do not or cannot provide support and endorsement. The more the teenager is valued and listened to at home, the more likely it is that the family will act as a protective factor.

All the elements that I mentioned in the early part of this book will contribute to protecting young people from the harm of risky behaviour. Where parents can provide limits and boundaries, where they are interested and involved, and where they are able to promote autonomy in an age-appropriate manner, the young person will be less likely to behave in a risky manner.

Of course this is not always the case. In the examples I will outline in the next section on challenging behaviour, the parents had done their best to support their teenagers. Other factors can play their part, and there are some teenagers who have a troubled time in spite of all the support offered by their families. However, broadly speaking what I have described as authoritative parenting (Chapter 6) leads to better outcomes for young people.

It is important to stress that parents are role models. In this sense it may not be what you say, but what you do that matters most. Teenagers are extremely sensitive to their parents' behaviour. They are also alert to anything that might be seen as hypocrisy. A parent who gives a lecture about safe drinking, but then has one too many pints in the pub, or one too many glasses of wine with a meal, is not going to have a positive influence on the teenager.

A parent's attitude to risk generally will also have an impact. When a parent ignores the speed limit when driving, the teenager sees an adult who takes risks. One study of young drug-takers showed an interesting finding. The parents of these young people were not themselves taking illegal drugs, but they were engaging in other types of risky behaviour. They were taking too many pills, or smoking too many cigarettes, or demonstrating a variety of other risky behaviours.

Teenagers are affected by the behaviour of their parents. In the best of circumstances parents are the most powerful protective factor against risk. However, if parents are risk-takers themselves they cannot expect their teenager to be immune from the influences of their behaviour.

There are, of course, other protective factors against risk. The school, the neighbourhood, and the friendship group can all play a part here. One good example of the protective role that friends can play comes from research on the impact of divorce. Studies have shown that teenagers adjust much better to divorce where the family does not move home. The reason for this is as follows. If the family moves, the young person will change school and lose their friendship group. If they stay put, they maintain the same friends. In many situations friends can offer the support needed to cope with the stress of divorce.

The school and the neighbourhood can also act as protective factors in relation to risky behaviour. A school that engages its students, and offers opportunities for all, will be less likely to have high levels of truancy or problem behaviour. A neighbourhood that provides resources for young people, such as sports clubs, youth clubs, and community centres, will reduce the likelihood that teenagers in the area will get into trouble.

To conclude this section, I should stress that many different factors play their part in protecting the young person from risk. The family is one of the most important of these, although in some circumstances even the most supportive families find themselves coping with serious and challenging behaviour. I will now turn to a consideration of this subject. At the end I will outline some of the lessons that can be learnt from the experiences of these parents.

Challenging behaviour

In this second section of the chapter I will look in some detail at three examples of seriously challenging behaviour. The three families I will highlight here were all interviewed by colleagues of mine, and have all given permission for their stories to be used. All names have been changed. As you will see they all faced troubled and troubling behaviour, and there are important lessons to be learnt from each example.

Anne's story

I couldn't cope with the long periods of total idleness when everyone else in the house is busy running about and doing jobs and your teenager is lying in bed all day. If you don't clean up their room it just gets to the point that the Council will come in and close it down. Also the long periods of depression were hard to cope with. Even though I can remember being depressed myself. I can remember also, not exactly enjoying it, one doesn't I suppose, but using my depression. I read tragic novels and dark poetry. For him there didn't seem to be that sort of outlet. He didn't seem to be able to do anything or find any energy to get out of his depression. He didn't go to school, and that was an enormous pressure on us all.

It's very, very difficult waking up in the morning and wondering if he's going to get up. If he gets up, is he going to school? If he goes to school is he going to register and then bunk off? Are they going to ring from school to say he's not there, or what he's done and this and that. The inevitable Education Welfare Officer knocks on your door, and you can't answer the questions they want answered. You don't know where he is. It's so hard when he's gone out and you hope he's in school. The weather's turning and you know he's walking around in a little jacket and standing in the park all day and he's up to something. That was tough. Tough for him and tough for us.

149

How have you dealt with it?

I don't feel I've dealt with it as adequately as I might. Perhaps on reflection one doesn't know how to deal with things. You're dealing with a human being who's not going to tell you anything about themselves, and a lot of times it's been like hitting your head on a brick wall. I haven't been consistent. I've been angry and then I've been loving and then I've been angry and then loving. I haven't liked the way I've done it, but I haven't known any other way because we're all suffering.

A lot of the time you feel it's being done to you deliberately. You think: "What have I done to you that you will do this to me?". That's the most painful bit. You start going back through your soul and asking: "When did I hurt him? When did I do those awful things that he's returning the act?". Of course he isn't, and it isn't you. He's just trying to tell you something and you're not understanding the words. I wish I had been a bit more consistent, but that's painful wishing.

It's brought out things in me that I never knew were there. I've got so angry, I wanted to kill him, I really did. Everybody laughs about it now, but it was true. I came home one day – I'd been to work and it was particularly stressful – and I thought he'd gone into school. Anyway I walked up the road, and he was sitting on this bench. My heart sank, and I thought: "Oh no, here we go again". I walked up to him and said: "Look, you promised me you'd go to school on Friday". He just looked at me, dead cocky, and said: "Yes, but I didn't tell you which Friday I was going".

My hands went for his throat. It was only that he was big and strong, because I chased him all down the road and kicked him and hit him and things. It was very public. I really wanted to hurt him. Afterwards he ran away, and stayed out. But that was violence I never knew I had. I'm not a violent person. I don't use violence, I don't need it. But you see … I phoned up the Educational Psychologist and told him what I'd done. He said: "He's got to know the limits to which he can push you, and now he's found it." I talked for an hour on the phone and that calmed me down a bit. It was just terrible.

How has it affected you personally?

> I've learnt a lot. I feel that, although as I've said I do have
> reasonable empathy and I try to remember what it was like
> to be a teenager, I've learnt a hell of a lot more about kids. I
> should really go and do counselling or something because I
> feel I could help and do something. I've got lots of nephews
> and nieces who are teenagers, and they are the ones who
> come to me. I can do things for them that I couldn't actually
> get hold of for my son when he needed me most.

Who or what helped you to cope?

> I have a very good sister-in-law and brother-in-law who
> have a wild teenager who's a year younger than my son. It
> was very nice to be able to share experiences with them.
> Since our kids became teenagers, whenever either one of
> them has got too heavy we've been able to unload onto the
> other one. So he has found his way to them, and their
> daughter has found her way to us. That's helped me to cope
> a lot.
> Whatever he did I think I've always believed in him. I've
> always believed he was capable and hoped it was only tem-
> porary that this was happening. I care about him too much
> to let him rot. But he's got to get off his backside and do
> things for himself. Sometimes you just need someone to give
> you a hand up. I've got a lot of faith in him, a lot.

What advice would you give someone else in a similar situation?

> Perhaps the first thing I can think of is: "Stay in there". Most
> children grow up to be OK, and there's no reason why,
> because you think yours is the worst, that he really is the
> worst. He probably isn't. Stick around, hang in there. He's
> an OK person. Try to listen to what they are really saying.
> That's the hardest thing in the world. It's the advice I'd give,
> but believe me I don't know how you take that advice,
> because you can do all the listening in the world and you
> can't hear what they are saying.

Susan's story

With my daughter the things that were most obvious were the constant missing money, and the odd personal behaviour. She had great difficulty with school. Although she wasn't low in intelligence, she couldn't get her life together after her GCSEs. She was always looking for things to be a bit more adventurous. Her whole life at that time was bits and pieces. She'd disappear for a few hours, and then come back. She'd sit in a chair and bat out, which means they go into a deep sleep. You try to wake her, and you're going back to excuses for your teenager. You think to yourself: "Well you know, she's got a headache, or she's had a bad night". You don't like her friends very much. The people she's mixing with aren't what you would consider people you thought she would mix with. She'd also make excuses for herself and you know that isn't correct.

When did you first notice the problem?

It was finding out things that you had suspicions of. Like if you have a teenager who you think might possibly be on drugs – it's finding out the things to look for. Like if someone is into heavy drugs the things to look out for are things like constant colds, constant blowing noses and also constantly missing money. Things disappearing from the house. Although you think they couldn't possibly be doing things like drinking too much or taking drugs, you think: "What else could it be?".

Of course you can't trust them. It is a very painful thing. You have to take your purse with you wherever you go. You take your purse to bed with you. It creates a nastiness really round the whole thing. The child you knew you could have taken her anywhere and felt safe, but the well-behaved child turns into someone you can't take to someone's house in case they go wandering off.

How did you deal with it all?

I tried to cover it up and pretend it wasn't happening. But eventually you can't cover it up. I sneaked out to the GP, without telling her. I asked for her to not be given any drugs, because they will abuse it. We looked everywhere for help, but there was nothing to give us that help that we needed. There was nothing, absolutely nothing. In the end she went to a particular clinic, but it was a bit of shock to me as it was a mental hospital, a very run-down mental hospital.

Although they did help her to get her drug-taking down in stages, I wasn't getting any help. I thought there was no one to help me in my thoughts. Because you feel so guilty as a parent. You think if I hadn't done this or I hadn't done that, would this have happened? The guilt is so heavy, and you need someone to say: "Stop thinking that way, because it's nothing that you have done. It happens to all types of families. It can happen to a child from a broken home. It can happen to a child in a very secure home". You need someone to help you when something like this happens.

How did it affect you personally?

It's made me more aware of how people behave. I always felt that I was to be ashamed of my daughter's behaviour. I always tried to cover it up outside the family by saying to the neighbours: "Oh, she's going through a bad patch" and make all the excuses why she was behaving the way she was. When it all came out I was so surprised by people's reactions. People aren't so unpleasant towards the problem. Usually you'll find that quite a few people have these problems, but hide them away. By hiding them away you become critical of yourself. If you open up and let people know, people are very kind.

Christine's story

My younger daughter rebelled at the age of 12 when she realised that she was adopted. Her father was ill, her grandfather had just died, and she loved him very much. She just felt alone. I think she felt I didn't have time for her. She was rejected by her natural mother and I was so busy coping with life. She rebelled so much that she started throwing temper tantrums and really becoming violent. Physically fighting with her elder sister, and then going out with her friends past the time I approved of. She was out every night. That was difficult to cope with. But she always came home. We thrashed things out. It took 2 years to go through that trauma – she thinking I didn't love her, and me thinking she didn't love me.

I went to the school, because she was missing school. They said they were busy and it was the social worker's job. For all that we were both interviewed by a social worker, and neither of us liked our private lives being pried into. My husband was quite ill at the time, and I was tired and I thought the best thing would be for me to get away for a week or so. I consulted the family doctor, and he agreed it would do us both a lot of good. We did get away for a fortnight's holiday, and when we came back my younger daughter felt that she did miss me. I felt my batteries were recharged, and I was more able to cope with the situation. We both decided we didn't want any more outside influence in the house. We did away with the social worker, and that was the beginning of getting closer again.

Conclusion

These three stories are striking for the degree of insight and wisdom they contain. Each mother has had to cope with some of the most difficult teenage behaviour imaginable, and yet all have learnt from their experiences. I will summarise some of the key points from these remarkable stories.

- Don't be afraid to share the problem, and to seek help. Being ashamed of what is happening is natural, but hiding the problem away does not help either the family or the teenager. Susan found that people were kind and helpful once they knew about her daughter's drug-taking.
- Remember you are not alone with this problem. It may feel as if your teenager is the worst teenager ever, but of course he or she is no such thing. Many other families will have problems, and if these can be shared things will be a lot easier to manage.
- A feeling of guilt is something that many parents experience. As Susan makes clear, guilt has to be tackled. Talk to someone about your feelings, and get them into perspective. It may feel as if the teenager is behaving badly to punish you, but this is not the root cause of the problem.
- Do make use of other adults if at all possible. Anne's experience of being able to help her nephews and nieces, while her in-laws

could help her own son, is striking. It is a good example of a parent being able to use a wider network of support outside the immediate family.

- Christine's story carries an important lesson. She was tired and stressed, and couldn't cope. She had a break from her daughter, and came back refreshed. That was an important turning point in their relationship.

- I was struck by Anne's statement: "He was trying to tell you something and you're not understanding the words". At the end of her story she suggests that you try to listen to what the teenager is really saying. This is very hard to do, but there is a lot of truth in it. Much of the troubled behaviour will be a communication about the pain and distress that the young person is experiencing.

- Finally, don't give up. As Anne says: "Whatever he did I think I've always believed in him. Stay around, hang in there. Never give up". Have faith in your teenager, and keep trying to find ways to help, either for the teenager or for yourself. If you give up, the teenager will be lost. If you hang in there, however hard it is, the teenager will come through. It may seem, as Susan says, that there is no help out there. But there will be someone, somewhere, who can offer help. Don't give up!

15

CONCLUSION

How parents can make use of the STAGE framework

I recently had a striking experience. I had given a lecture on young people's health to a group of professionals, and afterwards a small number came up to me. In a rather sheepish way they said: "I hope you don't mind us asking, but does anyone know how to be a good parent for a teenager?". They said that everyone knew how to be a parent of a toddler, but to be a parent of a teenager seemed like a mystery to them.

This led to a lively discussion. The questions these professionals asked have been very much in my mind while writing this book. I believe we do know a lot about what makes for effective parenting. Although we don't have all the answers, there are many things we do know. We know a lot about the needs of teenagers, and research has shown us that certain parenting styles lead to better outcomes. I have set out much of this learning in the course of the book.

In particular I have proposed the idea of STAGE, as I believe it provides a structure or framework for you to hang on to. This framework is based on well-respected research carried out in the last few years. STAGE identifies five key things about parenting. They are not the only elements of parenting, but they are five elements which are at the core of relationships between you and your teenager.

In a moment I will summarise these five elements, and show how you can make use of them. First, though, a brief word about the teenage years as a stage.

These years are best described as a stage for a number of good reasons.

- Transition. The teenage years are a transition from childhood to adulthood, and many of the puzzling things about teenage behaviour can be explained by recognising the idea of transition.

156

During transition the individual is neither one thing nor the other, and this is an unsettling place to be.

- Looking forward and looking back. The teenage years are a time when there is both anticipation for the possibilities of the future, but at times also a wish for the certainty and safety of childhood.
- Both child and adult. Inside every teenager is both a child and an adult. At times the young person is mature and independent, whereas at other times the needy child is in evidence.
- Major change in every area. During the teenage years the individual goes through more change than at any other time of life apart from the first three years. The brain matures in a major way, and this leads to alteration and upheaval in all spheres including the physical, intellectual, and emotional aspects of life. The impact of this should be recognised by young people and adults alike.
- A lot of learning is necessary. Because of the gradual transition to a new status, and because of all the changes that are happening, the young person has a lot to learn. No one gets things right the first time. Parents can do a huge amount to assist with this learning process.
- Change does not happen overnight. It may sometimes feel as if no change is happening at all. The teenage years are a very long stage, and much of the change will be slow, or invisible. Understanding this process of gradual change will help to make sense of the process.
- Teenage behaviour is a part of growing up. This behaviour is not designed to get at you, or hurt you, or push you away. It occurs partly as a result of changes in the brain, and partly as a way of dealing with the pressures and demands of a maturing process. This stage is a pathway to adulthood.

STAGE

It is now time to turn to the five elements of the STAGE framework. I will take each of the elements in turn, and summarise how you can make use of these ideas in your relationship with your teenager.

Significance

First, the S, which stands for the significance of parents. The key message here is that you matter. In spite of the fact that your teenager may send the opposite message, without your support and concern the young person will be lost. Just like the rest of us, teenagers need love. They need to be valued, they need to know they matter to their parents.

The idea of significance has a lot to do with your own self-confidence, your own self-esteem as a parent. You are important. Your role is as important now as it was when your son or daughter was three years old.

If you are feeling low, feeling that you are not doing a good enough job, remember that your teenager needs you.

If your teenager appears to be getting on fine without you, not asking for much from you, don't be fooled. Your teenager needs you.

If your teenager is pushing you away, telling you that you don't understand, don't let that put you off. Stay in there. Your teenager needs you.

Parents matter because of the climate they create in the home. The care, the interest, the concern that you show to your teenager are as vital as food and shelter.

Two-way communication

The T in STAGE stands for two-way communication. I emphasised earlier that communication involves both talking and listening. The two go hand in hand. I also underlined the two-way nature of relationships. I noted that the teenager's behaviour will influence you, but it works the other way around as well. The way you behave influences the young person. Indeed, the points I have just made about the significance of parents illustrate this nicely.

You will want to be able to communicate well with your teenager. Using the idea of two-way communication will help you do this.

Communication between you and your teenager is not you talking, or you asking questions, or "getting a result", as one parent put it.

It is not always easy to get a conversation going. It is not the same as talking to a friend. Be willing to stand back, and take your cue from the young person.

The young person will want to talk, but in a way that feels safe and secure. This means that you avoid interrogation, and that you respect the views of your teenager.

Remember the point about timing. Don't expect your teenager to talk at exactly the times that are good for you.

Sharing can help. It can sometimes be a good idea to talk a little about yourself. Don't embarrass your teenager by talking about intimate things. However, some sharing of your own experiences, or talking about what has happened to you during the day, can be a way of easing into a conversation.

Activities together can help. It is often easier to start talking when you are doing things with your teenager. This could be preparing food, doing something around the house, or enjoying a hobby. Doing things together takes the pressure off, and allows you both to chat in a more relaxed manner.

The young person will play as big a role in communication as you will. Be patient. Be willing to let the young person come to you in their own way. Make it clear you want to listen. That is the surest way to ensure that your teenager will want to talk.

Authority

The next topic is represented by the A, and concerns authority. The way you exercise your authority is central to everything else in your relationship with your teenager. There are many different ways that you can use your power with your teenager. You can be more or less responsive to the needs of your son or daughter. You can be more or less demanding in your expectations and in the boundaries and limits that you set. As I have noted earlier, the parenting style that offers the best environment for a teenager is called the "authoritative" style. Here the parent is loving and caring, as well as being firm in setting appropriate boundaries. The parent also promotes autonomy where possible, as well as identifying clear goals and expectations.

Getting as close as you can to an "authoritative" style will help you as well as helping your teenager.

Do not try and control everything in all areas of your teenager's life. Focus on a few important things, the things that really matter. If you are fighting over an untidy bedroom, ask yourself how much this matters in comparison with your teenager's safety or adjustment at school.

If you do have rules, make sure they can be explained so that they make sense to the young person. Where possible, negotiate rules so that they are agreed by everyone beforehand.

If you do feel you have to use discipline, try to make sure that the punishment is reasonable. Avoid anything that appears harsh or unfair. Be consistent and be clear about the justification for any punishment.

The way you exercise your authority will be affected by the way you and your partner work together. Where both mother and father are involved the parenting task is best described as co-parenting. You may not always be able to sing from the same song sheet, but it will be best to limit the amount of disagreement that you show in front of your teenager. Be prepared to back each other up, and show respect for each other. The more this happens, the more secure the teenager will feel.

There will be challenges. If there is a good reason for the limits you have set, then stick to your guns. The teenager may kick up a fuss, create a drama, say that you are ruining their life, but where possible you should remain firm. The experience of many parents before you is that, once things have calmed down, the young person will recognise that some firmness on your part was necessary.

Generation gap

The G represents the idea of a generation gap. By this I mean the possibility that you will judge your teenager based on your own experiences, rather than by the circumstances of today's generation. The idea of a generation gap can be helpful to you, as it will offer the opportunity of real dialogue with your teenager about what it is like growing up today. It is hardly a secret that things for young people are very different from the way they were 30 or 40 years ago. Taking this on board will make communication between you and your teenager a lot easier.

If you are making judgements about your teenager's behaviour, ask yourself what these judgements are based on. Are you being guided by what applied when you were growing up? If so, think again.

It is not always easy to respect another person's views if they clash with your own values. This is one of the reasons why parents and teenagers do not always see eye to eye, especially on things like sexual behaviour.

Disagreement is not a disaster. You can still have a good relationship even though you may not have the same ideas about things. The more you can be open to another point of view, the better your relationship with your teenager will be.

Emotion

Lastly, I come to the E, which stands for emotion. You will experience many emotions in your relationship with your teenager. You may feel angry, sad, rejected, upset, or worried. All these emotions and many more are part of being a parent of a teenager.

It is also important to recognise that your teenager will be experiencing a range of emotions, many of them new or confusing. During the teenage years it is often quite difficult for young people to manage and control their feelings. This naturally has its impact on you as a parent, so that at times both of you will be struggling with difficult feelings.

I want to emphasise that, by recognising your emotions, you will have a better chance of managing them. The more you can acknowledge your feelings, and get them into perspective, the easier it will be to have a warm relationship with your teenager.

If you are having a row with your teenager, you will be feeling angry and frustrated. Learn to take a step back. It can really help to walk away until you have both calmed down.

When there is a lot of emotion flying around, remember to use "I" statements as much as possible. It is so much better to say "I feel upset about what has happened" than to say "This is all your fault, you are the one to blame here". The more you accuse or blame the teenager, the harder it will be to communicate openly.

There may be times when it feels as if your teenager is getting at you, trying deliberately to make things difficult for you. It is more likely that the young person will be grappling with his or her own feelings of frustration or anger. So many parents say: remember they are not doing it to you.

When you are dealing with strong feelings, the other parent can play an extremely important role. It is here that the idea of parents as partners comes to the fore. If two parents, even when separated, can work together, the strong emotions are more likely to be put into perspective.

Try to get in touch with how you felt at the same age. As a teenager you will have struggled with your feelings, and no doubt you will have had a few difficult times with your own parents. It can help to remember these times.

Conclusion

- Look for the positives. Find ways to enjoy your teenager and to value their skills and capabilities.
- Praise is better than criticism. Try and keep a check on how much criticism you level at your teenager.
- Don't be afraid to set limits. Teenagers need a structure.
- Be clear about your expectations. If you don't state your expectations, how can a teenager know if they are getting it right? Your expectations are the guide to whether they are doing well or not.

- Teenagers need both parents. You may play different roles, but both mothers and fathers have key roles to play.
- Don't give up. If you are dealing with challenging behaviour, stick with it, however hard that may seem. Things will change. Keep the door open until the young person is able to come back to you.
- Finally, keep channels of communication open. This book has been written so that you will be able to keep talking to your teenager. Make use of the STAGE framework. If you do, I am hopeful that you will not need to ask: "Why won't my teenager talk to me?".

RESOURCES LIST

Section one

Books for parents of teenagers

Raising boys in the 21st century Steve Biddulph. Harper Collins. 2018. (An updated version of the worldwide best seller. Covers many issues that trouble parents today.)

The nature of adolescence: 4th edition John Coleman. Routledge. 2011. (A review of research findings covering all aspects of adolescent development.)

Teenagers translated: how to raise happy teens Janey Downshire and Naella Grew. Vermillion Press. 2014. (Written by two therapists, this provides useful insights into family life with teenagers. The aim of the book is to help parents promote resilient teens.)

Raise a happy teenager Suzie Hayman. Teach Yourself Books. 2010. (Written by a well-known agony aunt, this book offers an easy-to-read and practical approach to the challenges faced by parents of teenagers.)

Get out of my life, but first take me and Alex into town Tony Woolf and Suzanne Franks. Profile Books. 2011. (First published in America, this is described as a parent's guide to the new teenager. It is one book that has successfully crossed the Atlantic, and has become a bestseller in the UK.)

Section two

Books about the teenage brain

Inventing ourselves: the secret life of the teenage brain Sarah-Jayne Blakemore. Penguin Random House. 2018. (Written by one of the outstanding scientists in the UK, this easy to read book is a fascinating account of our current knowledge of the teenage brain.)

The teenage brain: a neuroscientist's survival guide to raising adolescents and young adults Frances Jensen. Harper Books. 2015. (As the title indicates, this is a book by a clinician using her knowledge to discuss how to be a parent of a teenager. This book comes from the US, but has been extremely popular in the UK.)

Blame my brain: the amazing teenage brain revealed Nicola Morgan. Walker Books. 2013. (This is the only book written specifically for teenagers. It includes quizzes and things for young people to do, and has become a bestseller. Very good for parents too.)

Section three

Websites

There are two general websites that can be highly recommended. The first, run by the charity Family Lives, covers all aspects of life with a teenager, including school and learning, behaviour, drugs and alcohol, on-line issues, sex, bullying, health and well-being, and how to talk to your teenager.

www.familylives.org.uk/advice/teenagers
Telephone helpline: 0808 800 2222

The second general website is part of NHS Choices, and goes under the title of Live Well. It covers everything related to young people and health, such as puberty, menstruation, sexual health, sleep, depression, eating, bullying, exercise, and so on. It also has a section on talking to your teenager, and a section to go to if you are worried about your teenager.

www.nhs.uk/conditions/stress-anxiety-depression/coping-with-your-teenager/?

Websites relating to bullying

There are many organisations which offer help on bullying matters. Both Family Lives and NHS Choices (Live Well) offer advice on this topic. In addition you could go to the following websites.

Childline
www.childline.org.uk/info-advice/bullying-abuse-safety/

Kidscape
www.kidscape.org.uk

Websites relating to drugs

In addition to the two general websites already mentioned there is an organisation called Talk to Frank, which is specifically designed to help with any problem concerning illegal drug use. There are sections on the website entitled: "Worried about a child" and "Advice for parents and carers".
www.talktofrank.com

Websites relating to eating disorders

The charity BEAT has a specific objective of providing advice and guidance on eating disorders. There is a section on the website for carers.

www.beateatingdisorders.org.uk

Websites relating to family matters

The charity Relate deals with divorce and separation, but also includes information on family matters generally. There is a section on the website for parents of teenagers.

www.relate.org.uk/relationship-help/

Gingerbread deals mainly with issues facing single parents, but has information about other aspects of family life as well.

www.gingerbread.org.uk

Divorce Aid has information about mediation and other aspects of family life following separation and divorce. There is a section providing advice for children, teenagers, and parents on questions to do with divorce.

www.divorceaid.co.uk

The Fatherhood Institute provides assistance for fathers in all aspects of their relationships with their children.

www.fatherhoodinstitute.org

Websites relating to legal matters

There is one organisation, the Coram Children's Legal Centre, which offers advice on legal matters where children and young people are concerned.

www.childrenslegalcentre.com

Websites relating to mental health

The charity Young Minds is one of the main organisations dealing with young people and mental health. It has a section on its website for parents and there is also a telephone helpline: 0808 802 5544.

https://youngminds.org.uk/find-help/for-parents/

Another organisation providing information on mental health issues for parents is the Royal College of Psychiatrists. The College provides a range of resources including factsheets on mental health and growing up.

www.rcpsych.ac.uk/healthadvice/parentsandyoungpeople.aspx

Websites relating to on-line safety

The organisation CEOP (Child Exploitation and Online Protection Centre) has a website which provides wide-ranging advice on on-line safety issues for young people.

www.thinkuknow.co.uk

Websites relating to sexual health

The two general websites mentioned at the beginning of this section have material on all aspects of sexual health. In addition, the charity Brook provides advice on everything to do with sexual health for those under the age of 25.

www.brook.org.uk

Section four

Novels about adolescence

To conclude this section on resources for parents, I will suggest six novels which I hope will provide as much pleasure for readers as they have done for me. I have not included the most celebrated novels about adolescence, such as *Catcher in the rye*. I will assume that most readers already know about books like this. My books are perhaps less well known, but each provides a memorable portrait of growing up in unusual circumstances.

The death of the heart Elizabeth Bowen. Published first in 1938, this book concerns a 16-year-old girl who loses her parents and is sent to live in London with unfeeling relatives. The book describes the confused yearnings of a teenage orphan, and her gradually increasing ability to take decisions for herself. It is a brilliant portrayal of the difficult emotions of adolescence.

A kestrel for a knave Barry Hines. A moving story of a working-class boy from the North of England who is troubled at school and at home. He finds comfort and escape by being able to train a kestrel. There is no happy ending, but the novel illustrates the resilience of young people. The book was made into a film *Kes*, which won widespread acclaim.

Who will run the frog hospital? Lorrie Moore. This book is set in Maine, in a small town close to the border with Quebec. It concerns two teenage girls, and their often painful journey towards maturity. Lorrie Moore is a poet, and the book contains some wonderful writing. The last two pages capture an extraordinary moment of harmony (both musical and emotional) between adolescent girls.

The member of the wedding Carson McCullers. At the heart of this novel are three phases of a weekend crisis in the life of a motherless 12-year-old girl in the Deep South of the USA. The author captures the heat and intensity of the summer, and the sense of growth and change experienced by the central character. This is a wonderful, almost luminous portrayal of early adolescence, with remarkable supporting characters. Once read, never forgotten.

American Pastoral Philip Roth. Set in the USA, in the politically charged atmosphere of the Vietnam War and the 1968 Presidential elections, this book will be seen as one of the classic novels of the twentieth century. Among the different themes it deals with, one has to do with an alienated teenager and her response to the social and family upheavals she witnesses as she grows up. She drops out of society, and the novel explores her behaviour and the reactions of her parents to her apparent rejection of everything they stand for.

The way I found her Rose Tremain. I am a great fan of Rose Tremain, and in this book she gives us an unforgettable portrait of a teenage boy's sexual awakening. With his mother he spends one summer in Paris and, left largely to his own devices, he explores the city. He meets adults who take him into an enchanting but mysterious world where he has to face many different challenges. It is a book of discovery, cleverly depicting the adolescent's journey from illusion to reality.

INDEX